Mrs Pepperpot's First Omnibus

BY THE SAME AUTHOR

Little Old Mrs Pepperpot
Mrs Pepperpot to the Rescue
Mrs Pepperpot Again
Mrs Pepperpot's Year
Mrs Pepperpot in the Magic Wood
Mrs Pepperpot's Outing

Mrs Pepperpot's First Omnibus
Mrs Pepperpot's Second Omnibus

Mrs Pepperpot's Busy Day
Mrs Pepperpot's Christmas

MRS PEPPERPOT'S FIRST OMNIBUS

Alf Prøysen

An omnibus consisting of:

Little Old Mrs Pepperpot
Mrs Pepperpot Again
Mrs Pepperpot to the Rescue

HUTCHINSON JUNIOR BOOKS

Hutchinson Junior Books Ltd
3 Fitzroy Square, London W1P 6JD

An imprint of the Hutchinson Publishing Group

London Melbourne Sydney Auckland
Wellington Johannesburg and agencies
throughout the world

This edition first published as
The Mrs Pepperpot Omnibus 1966
Seventh impression 1976
Eighth impression 1979

Printed in Great Britain by litho by The Anchor Press Ltd
and bound by Wm Brendon & Son Ltd
both of Tiptree, Essex

ISBN 0 09 127770 1

Little Old Mrs Pepperpot

and other stories

LITTLE OLD MRS PEPPERPOT

illustrated by

BJÖRN BERG

and other stories by ALF PRØYSEN

translated by Marianne Helweg

Contents

Little old Mrs. Pepperpot

THERE was once an old woman who went to bed at night as old women usually do, and in the morning she woke up as old women usually do. But on this particular morning she found herself shrunk to the size of a pepper-pot, and old women don't usually do that. The odd thing was, her name really was Mrs. Pepperpot.

'Well, as I'm now the size of a pepperpot, I shall have to make the best of it,' she said to herself, for she had no one else to talk to; her husband was out in the fields and all her children were grown up and gone away.

Now she happened to have a great deal to do that day. First of all she had to clean the house, then there was all the washing which was lying in soak and waiting to be done, and lastly she had to make pancakes for supper.

'I must get out of bed somehow,' she thought, and, taking hold of a corner of the eiderdown, she started rolling herself up in it. She rolled and rolled until the eiderdown was like a huge sausage, which fell softly on the floor. Mrs. Pepperpot crawled out and she hadn't hurt herself a bit.

The first job was to clean the house, but that was quite easy; she just sat down in front of a mouse-hole and squeaked till the mouse came out.

'Clean the house from top to bottom,' she said, 'or I'll tell the cat about you.' So the mouse cleaned the house from top to bottom.

Mrs. Pepperpot called the cat: 'Puss! Puss! Lick out all the plates and dishes or I'll tell the dog about you.' And the cat licked all the plates and dishes clean.

Then the old woman called the dog. 'Listen, dog; you make the bed and open the window and I'll give you a bone as a reward.' So the dog did as he was told, and when he had finished he sat down on the front door-step and waved his tail so hard he made the step shine like a mirror.

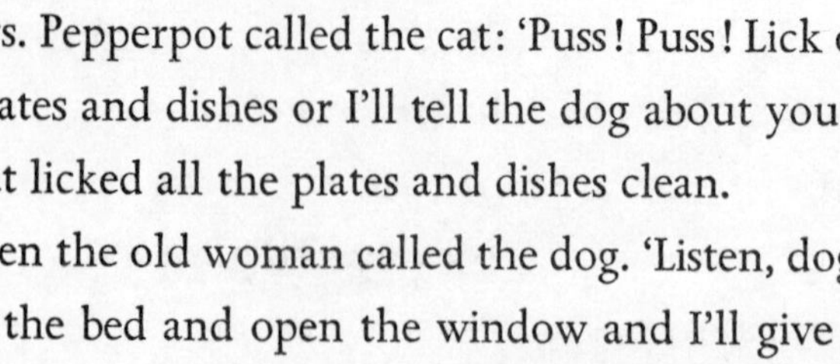

'You'll have to get the bone yourself,' said Mrs. Pepperpot, 'I haven't time to wait on people.' She pointed to the window-sill where a large bone lay.

After this she wanted to start her washing. She had put it to soak in the brook, but the brook was almost dry. So she sat down and started muttering in a discontented sort of way:

'I have lived a long time, but in all my born days I never saw the brook so dry. If we don't have a shower soon, I expect everyone will die of thirst.' Over and over again she said it, all the time looking up at the sky.

At last the raincloud in the sky got so angry that it decided to drown the old woman altogether. But she crawled under a monk's-hood flower, where she stayed snug and warm while the rain poured down and rinsed her clothes clean in the brook.

Now the old woman started muttering again: 'I have lived a long time, but in all my born days I have never known such a feeble South Wind as we have had lately. I'm sure if the South Wind started blowing this minute it couldn't lift me off the ground, even though I am no bigger than a pepperpot.'

The South Wind heard this and instantly came tearing along, but Mrs. Pepperpot hid in an empty badger set, and from there she watched the South Wind blow all the clothes right up on to her clothes-line.

Again she started muttering: 'I have lived a long time, but in all my born days I have never seen the sun give so little heat in the middle of the summer. It seems to have lost all its power, that's a fact.'

When the sun heard this it turned scarlet with rage and sent down fiery rays to give the old woman sunstroke. But by this time she was safely back in her house, and was sailing about the sink in a saucer. Meanwhile the furious sun dried all the clothes on the line.

'Now for cooking the supper,' said Mrs. Pepperpot; 'my husband will be back in an hour and, by hook or by crook, thirty pancakes must be ready on the table.'

She had mixed the dough for the pancakes in a bowl the day before. Now she sat down beside the bowl and said: 'I have always been fond of you, bowl, and I've told all the neighbours that there's not a bowl like you anywhere. I am sure, if you really wanted to, you could walk straight over to the cooking-stove and turn it on.'

And the bowl went straight over to the stove and turned it on.

Then Mrs. Pepperpot said: 'I'll never forget the day I bought my frying-pan. There were lots of pans in the shop, but I said: "If I can't have that pan hanging right over the shop assistant's head, I won't buy any pan at all. For that is the best pan in the whole world, and I'm sure if I were ever in trouble that pan could jump on to the stove by itself." '

And there and then the frying-pan jumped on to the stove. And when it was hot enough, the bowl tilted itself to let the dough run on to the pan.

Then the old woman said: 'I once read a fairy-tale about a pancake which could roll along the road. It was the stupidest story that ever I read. But I'm sure the pancake on the pan could easily turn a somersault in the air if it really wanted to.'

At this the pancake took a great leap from sheer pride and turned a somersault as Mrs. Pepperpot had said. Not only one pancake, but *all* the pancakes did this, and the bowl went on tilting and the pan went on frying until, before the hour was up, there were thirty pancakes on the dish.

Then Mr. Pepperpot came home. And, just as he opened the door, Mrs. Pepperpot turned back to her usual size. So they sat down and ate their supper.

And the old woman said nothing about having been as small as a pepperpot, because old women don't usually talk about such things.

Mrs. Pepperpot and the mechanical doll

IT WAS two days before Christmas. Mrs. Pepperpot hummed and sang as she trotted round her kitchen, she was so pleased to be finished with all her Christmas preparations. The pig had been killed, the sausages made, and now all she had to do was to brew herself a cup of coffee and sit down for a little rest.

'How lovely that Christmas is here,' she said, 'then everybody's happy—especially the children—that's the best of all; to see them happy and well.'

The old woman was almost like a child herself because of this knack she had of suddenly shrinking to the size of a pepperpot.

She was thinking about all this while she was making her coffee, and she had just poured it into the cup when there was a knock at the door.

'Come in,' she said, and in came a little girl who was oh! so pale and thin.

'Poor child! Wherever do you live—I'm sure I've never seen you before,' said Mrs. Pepperpot.

'I'm Hannah. I live in the little cottage at the edge of

the forest,' said the child, 'and I'm just going round to all the houses to ask if anybody has any old Christmas decorations left over from last year—glitter or paper-chains or glass balls or anything, you know. Have *you* got anything you don't need?'

'I expect so, Hannah,' answered Mrs. Pepperpot, and went up into the attic to fetch the cardboard box with all the decorations. She gave it to the little girl.

'How lovely! Can I really have all that?'

'You can,' said Mrs. Pepperpot, 'and you shall have something else as well. Tomorrow I will bring you a big doll.'

'I don't believe that,' said Hannah.

'Why not?'

'You haven't *got* a doll.'

'That's simple; I'll buy one,' said Mrs. Pepperpot. 'I'll bring it over tomorrow afternoon, but I must be home by six o'clock because it's Christmas Eve.'

'How wonderful if you can come tomorrow afternoon—I shall be all alone. Father and Mother both go out to work, you see, and they don't get back until the church bells have rung.'

So the little girl went home, and Mrs. Pepperpot went down to the toy-shop and bought a big doll. But when she woke up next morning there she was, once more, no bigger than a pepperpot.

'How provoking!' she said to herself. 'On this day of all days, when I have to take the doll to Hannah. Never mind! I expect I'll manage.'

After she had dressed she tried to pick up the doll, but it was much too heavy for her to lift.

'I'll have to go without it,' she thought, and opened the door to set off.

But oh dear! it had been snowing hard all night, and the little old woman soon sank deep in the snowdrifts. The cat was sitting in front of the house; when she saw something moving in the snow she thought it was a mouse and jumped on it.

'Hi, stop!' shouted Mrs. Pepperpot. 'Keep your claws to yourself! Can't you see it's just me shrunk again?'

'I beg your pardon,' said the cat, and started walking away.

'Wait a minute,' said Mrs. Pepperpot, 'to make up for your mistake you can give me a ride down to the main road.' The cat was quite willing, so she lay down and let the little old woman climb on her back. When they got to the main road the cat stopped. 'Can you hear anything?' asked Mrs. Pepperpot.

'Yes, I think it's the snow-plough,' said the cat, 'so we'll have to get out of the way, or we'll be buried in snow.'

'I don't want to get out of the way,' said Mrs. Pepperpot, and she sat down in the middle of the road and waited till the snow-plough was right in front of her; then she jumped up and landed smack on the front tip of the plough.

There she sat, clinging on for dear life and enjoying herself hugely. 'Look at me, the little old woman, driving the snow-plough!' she laughed.

When the snow-plough had almost reached the door of Hannah's little cottage, she climbed on to the edge nearest the side of the road and, before you could say Jack Robinson, she had landed safely on the great mound of snow thrown up by the plough. From there she could walk right across Hannah's hedge and slide down the other side. She was shaking the snow off her clothes on the doorstep when Hannah came out and picked her up.

'Are you one of those mechanical dolls that you wind up?' asked Hannah.

'No,' said Mrs. Pepperpot, 'I am a woman who can wind myself up, thank you very much. Help me brush off all the snow and then let's go inside.'

'Are you perhaps the old woman who shrinks to the size of a pepperpot?'

'Of course I am, silly.'

'Where's the doll you were going to bring me?' asked Hannah when they got inside.

'I've got it at home. You'll have to go back with me and fetch it. It's too heavy for me.'

'Shouldn't you have something to eat, now that you've come to see me? Would you like a biscuit?' And the little girl held out a biscuit in the shape of a ring.

'Thank you very much,' said Mrs. Pepperpot and popped her head through the biscuit ring.

Oh, how the little girl laughed! 'I quite forgot you were so small,' she said; 'let me break it into little pieces so that you can eat it.' Then she fetched a thimble and filled it with fruit juice. 'Have a drink,' she said.

'Thank you,' said Mrs. Pepperpot.

After that they played a lot of good games; ride-a-cock-horse with Mrs. Pepperpot sitting on Hannah's knee, and hide-and-seek. But the little girl had an awful time trying to find Mrs. Pepperpot—she hid in such awkward places. When they had finished playing Hannah put on her coat and with Mrs. Pepperpot in her pocket she went off to fetch her beautiful big doll.

'Oh, thank you!' she exclaimed when she saw it. 'But do you know,' she added, 'I would really rather have *you* to play with all the time.'

'You can come and see me again if you like,' said Mrs. Pepperpot, 'I am often as small as a pepperpot, and then it's nice to have a little help around the house. And, of course, we can play games as well.'

So now the little girl often spends her time with Mrs. Pepperpot. She looks ever so much better, and they often talk about the day Mrs. Pepperpot arrived on the snow-plough, and about the doll she gave Hannah.

Mr. Pepperpot buys macaroni

'IT'S a very long time since we've had macaroni for supper,' said Mr. Peppercot one day.

'Then you shall have it today, my love,' said his wife. 'But I shall have to go to the grocer for some. So first of all you'll have to find me.'

'Find you?' said Mr. Pepperpot. 'What sort of nonsense is that?' But when he looked round for her he couldn't see her anywhere. 'Don't be silly, wife,' he said; 'if you're hiding in the cupboard you must come out this minute. We're too big to play hide-and-seek.'

'*I'm* not too big, I'm just the right size for "hunt-the-pepperpot",' laughed Mrs. Pepperpot. 'Find me if you can!'

'I'm not going to charge round my own bedroom looking for my wife,' he said crossly.

'Now, now! I'll help you; I'll tell you when you're warm. Just now you're very cold.' For Mr. Pepperpot was peering out of the window, thinking she might have jumped out. As he searched round the room she called out 'Warm!', 'Colder!', 'Getting hotter!' until he was quite dizzy.

At last she shouted, 'You'll burn the top of your bald head if you don't look up!' And there she was, sitting on the bedpost, swinging her legs and laughing at him.

Her husband pulled a very long face when he saw her. 'This is a bad business—a very bad business,' he said, stroking her cheek with his little finger.

'I don't think it's a bad business,' said Mrs. Pepperpot.

'I shall have a terrible time. The whole town will laugh when they see I have a wife the size of a pepperpot.'

'Who cares?' she answered. 'That doesn't matter a bit. Now put me down on the floor so that I can get ready to go to the grocer and buy your macaroni.'

But her husband wouldn't hear of her going; he would go to the grocer himself.

'That'll be a lot of use!' she said. 'When you get home you'll have forgotten to buy the macaroni. I'm sure even if I wrote "macaroni" right across your forehead you'd bring back cinnamon and salt herrings instead.'

'But how are you going to walk all that way with those tiny legs?'

'Put me in your coat pocket; then I won't need to walk.'

There was no help for it, so Mr. Pepperpot put his wife in his pocket and set off for the shop.

Soon she started talking: "My goodness me, what a lot of strange things you have in your pocket—screws and nails, tobacco and matches—there's even a fish-hook! You'll have to take that out at once; I might get it caught in my skirt.'

'Don't talk so loud,' said her husband as he took out the fish-hook. 'We're going into the shop now.'

It was an old-fashioned village store where they sold everything from prunes to coffee cups. The grocer was particularly proud of the coffee cups and held one up for Mr. Pepperpot to see. This made his wife curious and she popped her head out of his pocket.

'You stay where you are!' whispered Mr. Pepperpot.

'I beg your pardon, did you say anything?' asked the grocer.

'No, no, I was just humming a little tune,' said Mr. Pepperpot. 'Tra-la-la!'

'What colour are the cups?' whispered his wife. And her husband sang:

'The cups are blue
With gold edge too,
But they cost too much
So that won't do!'

After that Mrs. Pepperpot kept quiet—but not for long. When her husband pulled out his tobacco tin she couldn't resist hanging on to the lid. Neither her husband nor anyone else in the shop noticed her slipping on to the counter and hiding behind a flour-bag. From there she darted silently across to the scales, crawled under them, past a pair of kippers wrapped in newspaper, and found herself next to the coffee cups.

'Aren't they pretty!' she whispered, and took a step backwards to get a better view. Whoops! She fell right into the macaroni drawer which had been left open. She hastily covered herself up with macaroni, but the grocer heard the scratching noise and quickly banged the drawer shut. You see, it did sometimes happen that mice got in the drawers, and that's not the sort of thing you want people to know about, so the grocer pretended nothing had happened and went on serving.

There was Mrs. Pepperpot all in the dark; she could hear the grocer serving her husband now. 'That's good,' she thought. 'When he orders macaroni I'll get my chance to slip into the bag with it.'

But it was just as she had feared; her husband forgot what he had come to buy. Mrs. Pepperpot shouted at the top of her voice, 'MACARONI!', but it was impossible to get him to hear.

'A quarter of a pound of coffee, please,' said her husband.

'Anything else?' asked the grocer.

'MACARONI!' shouted Mrs. Pepperpot.

'Two pounds of sugar,' said her husband.

'Anything more?'

'MACARONI!' shouted Mrs. Pepperpot.

But at last her husband remembered the macaroni of his own accord. The grocer hurriedly filled a bag. He thought he felt something move, but he didn't say a word.

'That's all, thank you,' said Mr. Pepperpot. When he got outside the door he was just about to make sure his

wife was still in his pocket when a van drew up and offered to give him a lift all the way home. Once there he took off his knapsack with all the shopping in it and put his hand in his pocket to lift out his wife.

The pocket was empty.

Now he was really frightened. First he thought she was teasing him, but when he had called three times and still no wife appeared, he put on his hat again and hurried back to the shop.

The grocer saw him coming. 'He's probably going to complain about the mouse in the macaroni,' he thought.

'Have you forgotten anything, Mr. Pepperpot?' he asked, and smiled as pleasantly as he could.

Mr. Pepperpot was looking all round. 'Yes,' he said.

'I would be very grateful, Mr. Pepperpot, if you would keep it to yourself about the mouse being in the macaroni. I'll let you have these fine blue coffee cups if you'll say no more about it.'

'Mouse?' Mr. Pepperpot looked puzzled.

'Shh!' said the grocer, and hurriedly started wrapping up the cups.

Then Mr. Pepperpot realized that the grocer had mistaken his wife for a mouse. So he took the cups and rushed home as fast as he could. By the time he got there he was in a sweat of fear that his wife might have been squeezed to death in the macaroni bag.

'Oh, my dear wife,' he muttered to himself. 'My poor darling wife. I'll never again be ashamed of you being the size of a pepperpot—as long as you're still alive!'

When he opened the door she was standing by the cooking-stove, dishing up the macaroni—as large as life; in fact, as large as you or I.

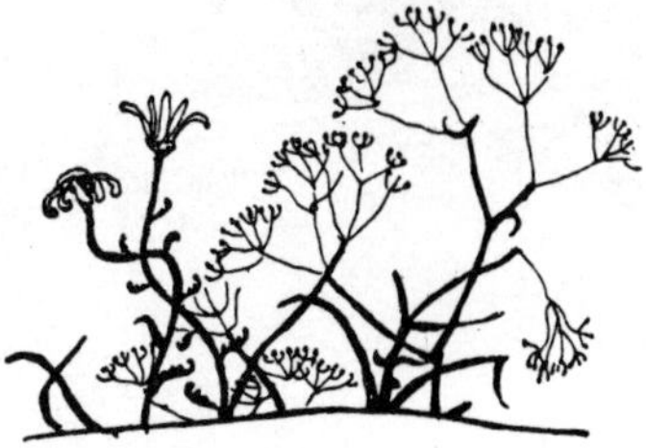

Queen of the Crows

DID you know that the woman who was as small as a pepperpot was queen of all the crows in the forest?

No, of course you didn't, because it was a secret between Mrs. Pepperpot and me until now. But now I'm going to tell you how it happened.

Outside the old woman's house there was a wooden fence and on it used to sit a large crow.

'I can't understand why that crow has to sit there staring in at the kitchen window all the time,' said Mr. Pepperpot.

'I can't imagine,' said Mrs. Pepperpot. 'Shoo! Get along with you!'

But the crow didn't move from the fence.

Then one day Mrs. Pepperpot had her shrinking turn again (I can't remember now what she was supposed to be doing that day, but she was very busy), and by the time she had clambered over the doorstep she was quite out of breath.

'Oh dear, it's certainly hard to be so small,' she puffed.

Suddenly there was a sound of flapping wings and the

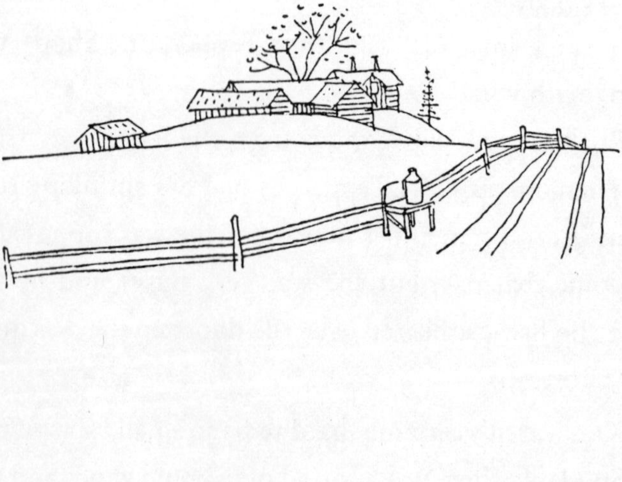

crow swooped down, picked up Mrs. Pepperpot by her skirt and flew up over the highest fir trees in the forest with her.

'What's the idea, may I ask? You wait till I'm back to my proper size and I'll beat you with my birch rod and chase you off for good!'

'Caw-caw! You're small enough now, at any rate,' said the crow; 'I've waited a long time for this. I saw you turn small once before, you see, so I thought it might happen again. And here we are, but only just in time. Today is the Crows' Festival and *I'm* to be Queen of the Crows!'

'If you're to be Queen of the Crows, you surely don't need to take an old woman like me along?'

'That's just where you're wrong,' said the crow, and flapped her wings; the old woman was heavier than she had expected. 'Wait till we get back to my nest, then you'll see why.'

'There's not much else I *can* do,' thought poor Mrs. Pepperpot as she dangled from the crow's claws.

'Here we are; home!' said the crow, and dropped Mrs. Pepperpot into the nest. 'Lucky it's empty.'

'It certainly is; I fell right on a spiky twig and grazed my shinbone.'

'Poor little thing!' said the crow. 'But look, I've made you a lovely bed of feathers and down. You'll find the down very snug and warm, and the feathers are just the thing when night falls and the wind begins to blow.'

'What do I want with feathers and down?'

'I want you to lie down and go to sleep,' said the crow. 'But first you must lend me your clothes. So please take off your head-scarf now, and your blouse and your skirt.

'The scarf I want you to tie round my neck, the skirt goes on one wing and the blouse on the other. Then I shall fly to the clearing in the forest where all the crows are meeting for the Festival. The finest-looking crow will be chosen queen, and that's going to be me! When I win I'll think of you. Caw-caw!'

'Well, if you think you'll be any better looking in my old clothes, you're welcome,' said Mrs. Pepperpot as she dressed up the crow.

'Hurry, hurry!' said the crow. 'There's another crow living over there in that fir tree on the hill. She'll be dropping in here on her way; we were going to the Festival together. But now that I'm all dressed up I'd rather go alone. Caw-caw-caw!' And off she flew.

Mrs. Pepperpot sat shivering in her petticoat, but then she thought of burrowing deep under the feathers and down as the crow had told her to do, and she found she was soon warm and cosy.

Suddenly the whole branch started swaying, and on the end perched a huge crow.

'Mary Crow, are you at home?' croaked the crow, sidling up and poking her big beak over the edge of the nest.

'Mary Crow has gone to the Festival,' said Mrs. Pepperpot.

'Then who are you, who are you?' asked the crow.

'I'm just an old woman shivering with cold, because Mary Crow has borrowed my clothes.'

'Caw-caw! Oh blow! She'll be the finest-looking crow at the Festival,' shrieked the crow as she threw herself into the air from the branch. 'But I'll have the scarf off her!'

Mrs. Pepperpot lay down to sleep again. Suddenly she rolled right over into the corner of the nest, the branch was shaking so much.

'That'll be another crow,' she thought, and quite right, it was; the biggest crow she had ever seen was swinging on the tip of the branch.

'Mary Crow, Mary Crow, have you seen Betty Crow?'

'I've seen both Mary Crow *and* Betty Crow,' said Mrs. Pepperpot.

'Who are you, who are you?' squawked the crow.

'I'm just an old woman shivering with cold because Mary Crow has borrowed my clothes.'

'Caw-caw! What a bore! Now Mary Crow will be the best-looking crow.'

'I'm not so sure about that,' said the old woman, 'because Betty Crow flew after Mary Crow and was going to have the scarf off her.'

'I'll take the skirt, I'll take the skirt!' croaked the biggest crow, and took off from the branch with such a bound that Mrs. Pepperpot had to hold on tight not to get thrown out of the nest.

In the clearing in the forest there were lots and lots of crows. They sat round in a circle and, one by one, they hopped into the middle to show themselves. Some of the crows could hop on one leg without touching the ground with their wings. Others had different kinds of tricks, and the crows sitting round had to choose the best one to be their queen.

At last there were only three crows left. They sat well away from each other, polishing their feathers and looking very fierce indeed. One had a scarf, the second had a skirt and the third had a blouse. So you can guess which crows *they* were. One of them was to be chosen queen.

'The crow with the scarf round her neck is the best,' said some of the crows, 'she looks most like a human being.'

'No, no; the crow with the skirt looks best!'

'Not at all! The crow with the blouse looks most dignified, and a queen should be dignified.'

Suddenly something fell with a bump to the ground; the jay had arrived right in the middle of the Festival with a strange-looking bird in its beak.

'Caw-caw! The jay has no business to be here!' croaked all the crows.

'I won't stay a minute,' said the jay. 'I've just brought you your queen!' and he flew off.

All the crows stared at the strange little raggedy bird in the middle of the ring. They could see it was covered in crow's feathers and down, but raggedy crows could not be allowed at the Festival.

'It's against the law!' said the biggest crow.

'Let's peck it, let's peck it!' said Mary Crow.

'Yes, let's hack it to pieces!' said Betty Crow.

'Yes, yes!' croaked all the crows. 'We can't have raggedy birds here!'

'Wait a minute!' said the raggedy bird, and climbed on to a tree-stump. 'I'll sing you a song.' And before they could stop it, it started singing 'Who Killed Cock Robin?' And it knew all the verses. The crows were delighted; they clapped and flapped their wings till the raggedy bird lost nearly all its feathers.

'D'you know any more? D'you know any more?' they croaked.

'I can dance the polka,' said the raggedy bird, and danced round the circle till they were all out of breath.

'You shall be our Queen!' they all shouted. 'Four Court Crows will carry you wherever you wish to go.'

'How wonderful!' laughed the Queen of the Crows. 'Then they must carry me to the house over there by the edge of the forest.'

'What would Your Majesty like to wear?'

'I would like to wear a skirt, a blouse and a head-scarf,' said the Queen.

Much later that night there was a knock at the cottage door. Mr. Pepperpot opened it, and there stood his wife.

'You're very late, wife,' he said. 'Where have you been?'

'I've been to a Festival,' she answered.

'But why are you covered in feathers?'

'You just go to bed and don't trouble yourself,' said Mrs. Pepperpot. She went over and stuck a feather in the corner of the window.

'Why do you do that?' asked her husband.

'For no reason at all.'

But she really did it because she had been chosen Queen of the Crows.

Mrs. Pepperpot at the bazaar

ONE day Mrs. Pepperpot was alone in her kitchen. At least, she was not *quite* alone, because Hannah, the little girl who had had the doll for Christmas, was there as well. She was busy scraping out a bowl and licking the spoon, for the old woman had been making gingerbread shapes.

There was a knock at the door. Mrs. Pepperpot said, 'Come in.' And in walked three very smart ladies.

'Good afternoon,' said the smart ladies. 'We are collecting prizes for the lottery at the school bazaar this evening. Do you think you have some little thing we could have? The money from the bazaar is for the boys' brass band—they need new instruments.'

'Oh, I'd like to help with that,' said Mrs. Pepperpot, for she dearly loved brass bands. 'Would a plate of gingerbread be any use?'

'Of course,' said the smart ladies, but they laughed behind her back. 'We could take it with us now if you have it ready,' they said. But Mrs. Pepperpot wanted to go to the bazaar herself, so she said she would bring the gingerbread.

So the three smart ladies went away and Mrs. Pepperpot was very proud and pleased that she was going to a bazaar.

Hannah was still scraping away at the bowl and licking the sweet mixture from the spoon.

'May I come with you?' she asked.

'Certainly, if your father and mother will let you.'

'I'm sure they will,' said the child, 'because Father has to work at the factory and Mother is at her sewing all day.'

'Be here at six o'clock then,' said Mrs. Pepperpot, and started making another batch of gingerbread shapes.

But when Hannah came back at six the old woman was not there. All the doors were open, so she went from room to room, calling her. When she got back to the kitchen she heard an odd noise coming from the table. The mixing bowl was upside down, so she lifted it carefully. And there underneath sat her friend who was now again as small as a pepperpot.

'Isn't this a nuisance?' said Mrs. Pepperpot. 'I was just cleaning out the bowl after putting the gingerbread in the oven when I suddenly started shrinking. Then the bowl turned over on me. Quick! Get the cakes out of the oven before they burn!'

But it was too late; the gingerbread was burnt to a cinder.

Mrs. Pepperpot sat down and cried, she was so disappointed. But she soon gave that up and started thinking instead. Suddenly she laughed out loud and said:

'Hannah! Put me under the tap and give me a good wash. We're going to the bazaar, you and I!'

'But you can't go to the bazaar like that!' said Hannah.

'Oh yes, I can,' said Mrs. Pepperpot, 'as long as you do what I say.'

Hannah promised, but Mrs. Pepperpot gave her some very queer orders. First she was to fetch a silk ribbon and tie it round the old woman so that it looked like a skirt. Then she was to fetch some tinsel from the Christmas decorations. This she had to wind round and round to make a silver bodice. And lastly she had to make a bonnet of gold foil.

'Now you must wrap me carefully in cellophane and put me in a cardboard box,' said Mrs. Pepperpot.

'Why?' asked Hannah.

'When I've promised them a prize for the bazaar they must have it,' said Mrs. Pepperpot, 'so I'm giving them myself. Just put me down on one of the tables and say you've brought a mechanical doll. Tell them you keep the key in your pocket and then pretend to wind me up so that people can see how clever I am.'

Hannah did as she was told, and when she got to the

bazaar and put the wonderful doll on the table, many people clapped their hands and crowded round to see.

'What a pretty doll!' they said. 'And what a lovely dress!'

'Look at her gold bonnet!'

Mrs. Pepperpot lay absolutely still in her cardboard box, but when she heard how everybody praised her, she winked at Hannah with one eye, and Hannah knew what she wanted. She lifted Mrs. Pepperpot very carefully out of the box and pretended to wind her up at the back with a key.

Everyone was watching her. But when Mrs. Pepperpot began walking across the table, picking her way through the prizes, there was great excitement.

'Look, the doll can walk!'

And when Mrs. Pepperpot began to dance they started shouting and yelling with delight, 'The doll is dancing!'

The three smart ladies who had been to see Mrs. Pepperpot earlier in the day sat in special seats and looked very grand. One of them had given six expensive coffee cups, the second an elegant table mat and the third a beautiful iced layer cake.

Mrs. Pepperpot decided to go over and speak to them, for she was afraid they had recognized her and thought it queer that she hadn't brought the gingerbread.

The three smart ladies were very pleased when the doll came walking across the table to them.

'Come to me!' said the one who had given the coffee cups, and stretched her hand out towards Mrs. Pepperpot, who walked on to it obediently.

'Let me hold her a little,' said the lady with the elegant table mat, and Mrs. Pepperpot went over to her hand.

'Now it's my turn,' said the lady with the iced cake.

'I'm sure they know it's me,' thought Mrs. Pepperpot, 'that's why they stare at me so hard and hold me on their hands.'

But then the lady with the cake said, 'Well, I must say, this is a much better prize than the gingerbread that the odd old woman offered us today.'

Now she should never have said that; Mrs. Pepperpot leaped straight out of her hand and landed PLOP! right in the middle of the beautiful iced layer cake. Then she got up and waded right through it. The cake lady screamed, but people were shouting with laughter by now.

'Take that doll away!' shrieked the second lady, but *squish, squash!* went Mrs. Pepperpot's sticky feet, right across her lovely table mat.

'Get that dreadful doll away!' cried the third lady. But it was too late; Mrs. Pepperpot was on the tray with

the expensive coffee cups, and began to dance a jig. Cups and saucers flew about and broke in little pieces.

What a-to-do! The conductor of the brass band had quite a job to quieten them all down. He announced that the winning numbers of the lottery would be given out.

'First prize will be the wonderful mechanical doll,' he said.

When Hannah heard that she was very frightened. What would happen if somebody won Mrs. Pepperpot, so that she couldn't go home to her husband? She tugged at Mrs. Pepperpot's skirt and whispered, 'Shall I put you in my pocket and creep away?'

'No,' said Mrs. Pepperpot.

'But think how awful it would be if someone won you and took you home.'

'What must be must be!' said Mrs. Pepperpot.

The conductor called out the winning number, '311!' Everyone looked at their tickets, but no one had number 311.

'That's a good thing!' sighed Hannah with relief. There would have to be another draw. But just then she remembered she had a ticket in her hand; it was number 311!

'Wait!' she cried, and showed her ticket. The conductor looked at it and saw it was the right one.

So Hannah was allowed to take Mrs. Pepperpot home.

Next day the old woman was her proper size again and Hannah only a little girl, and Mrs. Pepperpot said, 'You're my little girl, aren't you?'

'Yes,' said Hannah, 'and you're my very own Mrs. Pepperpot, because I won you at the bazaar yesterday.'

And that was the end of Mrs. Pepperpot's adventures for a very long time.

Mr. Puffblow's hat

THERE was once a man called Mr. Puffblow who had an enormous hat. Mr. Puffblow was a very severe sort of man, and when he walked down the street he used to get very angry indeed if any of the children stared at his hat. And if they as much as stopped and looked at the house where he lived he would rush out and chase them off, because he thought they wanted to steal his apples.

Nobody dared go against Mr. Puffblow. 'Ssh!' mothers would say to their children playing in the street. 'You'd better be quiet–Mr. Puffblow is coming this way!'

Every day at precisely half past eleven Mr. Puffblow walked down the street to fetch his pint of milk from the dairy. So, until *that* was over, everybody stayed indoors.

One day the West Wind came tearing through the town, and I don't think there is anything like the West Wind for upsetting things in the autumn; the mischief it gets up to is nobody's business.

Now suddenly the West Wind caught sight of Mr.

Puffblow walking down the street with his enormous hat on.

'Wheee!' said the West Wind. 'That's just the hat for me!'

So, with a puff and a blow, it tipped Mr. Puffblow's hat off his head.

The hat bowled along the pavement. Mr. Puffblow ran after it. But just as he was about to catch it, the West Wind pounced and blew it further away. This game went on for a long time until at last the West Wind carried the hat high up into the air, right over the rooftops of the town to the wood beyond.

'I'm tired of playing with you now,' said the West

Wind to the hat. 'I'm going to drop you in this brook and leave you to sink or swim. Good luck!'

The hat turned two more somersaults in the air, then plopped into the brook and floated away like a little round ship.

It so happened that a tiny fieldmouse had been out in the wood that day gathering nuts, and he had fallen into the brook. He could swim all right, but the current was so strong he was almost drowned struggling against it.

When he saw the hat sailing past he caught hold of the brim with his paws and clambered up to the top of the crown.

'This would make a very good ship,' thought the

fieldmouse. 'I wish some of the other mice could see me now.' And he gave a loud squeak.

Sure enough, another fieldmouse heard him, and when he saw the fine-looking ship he called the other mice, and in the end there were eight little fieldmice sailing along on the hat. The one who got on first was the captain, the second was his mate and the rest were the crew.

You have no idea what fun those fieldmice had with Mr. Puffblow's hat that autumn! Every day they went for a sail, and when winter came and it got too cold, they dragged the hat on to dry land and used it for a house. All through the winter they sat inside it, snug and warm, telling each other mouse fairy-tales and singing mouse carols at Christmas.

And when spring came they started sailing again.

Then one day there was a great noise and to-do in the wood. A whole crowd of children from the town were out for a picnic. There was a man with them and they were all laughing and shouting and having a fine time together. The man carried the smallest one on his shoulders while the others were clinging to his coat-tails. They picked flowers for him and showed him all the nicest things they could find in the wood on a spring day.

Suddenly they stopped by the brook. 'Look over there!' cried one of the children. 'Look at that big hat on the other bank!'

The mice had just dragged the hat out of the brook because they were going home to supper.

When the man saw the hat he laughed and laughed. Because, you see, he knew it.

Can you guess who he was? Mr. Puffblow! But a very much nicer Mr. Puffblow now, and do you know why? Well, when he used to wear that enormous hat on his head he was always afraid the children would laugh at him. But from the moment he lost the hat he became quite different; he was no longer afraid.

'There's your old hat, Mr. Puffblow!' shouted the children with glee. 'Don't you want to wear it again?'

'Certainly not!' said Mr. Puffblow. 'Come along now, children, let's pick anemones.'

So they did.

And the fieldmice are using Mr. Puffblow's hat for a ship to this day.

Miriam-from-America

THERE was once a doll who was so beautifully smart that she had to sit all day, every day, on top of a chest of drawers. She couldn't *do* anything, not even shut her eyes or stand on her feet, and her fine silk dress was sewn on to her body, so she couldn't be undressed. But there was no doubt about it; she was the grandest of all the dolls just because she sat on top of the chest of drawers.

The little girl who owned the doll never allowed her school friends to touch her. When they asked why they mustn't touch her, the little girl said:

'Don't you know that this doll is called Miriam and comes from America? What's more, she's crossed the Atlantic in a ship, and even *I*'m not allowed to touch her till I'm a big girl.'

When her friends heard this their eyes grew round with astonishment and, putting their hands behind their backs, they stood and stared at Miriam-from-America.

One day the window near the chest of drawers stood

open, and someone opened the door as well so that there was a draught. This blew Miriam off the chest straight out of the window into the garden below. There she lay, quite still, looking up at the sky.

It grew darker and darker, until it was late night and the stars began to twinkle. All at once, the full moon came sailing across the sky.

'What is that strange-looking thing in the garden?' said the moon, and turned his light on Miriam.

Miriam said nothing; she just went on lying there. But the wind whistled in the tree tops and answered for her: 'That is Miriam-from-America. She is the most elegant doll because she usually sits right on top of a chest of drawers.'

'Can't she speak for herself?' asked the moon.

'I don't think so,' said the wind. 'Can you talk, Miriam?'

Miriam said nothing.

'Try and talk to us—just a little,' said the moon.

Miriam still didn't move, but the moon saw she wanted to say something, so he waited.

'Over the sea and under the sky!' Miriam said suddenly.

'Why do you say "over the sea and under the sky"?' asked the moon.

'Because I have sailed over the sea,' said Miriam, 'and I thought that was great fun. And now I'm lying under the sky and that is even more fun.'

'But I suppose sitting on a chest of drawers being the most elegant, the most beautiful, doll is more fun still?' said the wind.

'It's the dullest thing in the world!' said Miriam. 'Couldn't you two help me so that I don't have to be so elegant, so smart, any more?'

'That's easy,' said the wind, and blew Miriam straight into a big puddle. Miriam laughed; it was lovely to splash about in water. She had never tried that before.

'I must help too,' said the moon, and he threw a beam of light on the kennel where the dog Rover lay asleep. He woke up at once and saw Miriam lying in the puddle. So he took her smart silk dress between his

teeth and ran down the road with her. Miriam was jolted up and down, but she didn't mind a bit because she knew Rover well; she had often seen him from her chest of drawers when he lay curled up by the fire. And now here she was, having a lovely game with him!

The moon followed them down the street, and so did the wind, turning somersaults all the way. At last they came back to the house where Miriam lived. But how was she to get indoors again? The window was still open but Miriam couldn't possibly climb up to it.

'We shall have to ask the crow to carry her up in his beak,' said the moon. So they did. The crow was very ready to help. He flew through the window with Miriam and set her down on the chest of drawers.

Well, you can imagine the fuss there was next day when the little girl's mother saw what a mess Miriam was in! But the little girl was very pleased, because from now on she could play with Miriam as much as she liked. She took her for rides in the doll's pram, and every time the wind blew Miriam waved her hand—just a little bit. This was supposed to mean:

'Thank you, wind, for helping me get away from the chest of drawers!'

Jumping Jack and his friends

THE things I am going to tell you about in this story only happened last night. They happened after everyone had gone to bed; not only the little children and the big children, but the grown-ups as well.

In a shed—an ordinary kind of garden shed which people use for bicycles and shovels and rakes and spades—lived a family of toys.

There was a tricycle, a skipping rope hanging on a nail and two hop-scotch stones stuck in a crack in the floor. Almost hidden, stood a little red wheelbarrow which the children used in the sand pit, and in it lay a ball and a jumping jack. This jumping jack was so smart he had his name painted across his back in big letters: JUMPING JACK.

The toys had been in the shed all winter. They had seen the snowdrifts when the grown-ups came for shovels to clear the paths, and they had heard the wind howl and sigh. But just lately the toys had heard a new noise—a slow *drip . . . drip . . .* from the roof. Then it had turned into *drippy-drippy-drop* and at last a very quick *drip,*

drip, drip, drip, and they knew that all the snow had melted from the roof.

'Are we going out now?' asked Jumping Jack, who had never seen winter before.

'Not for a long time yet,' answered the Wheelbarrow.

One day a little boy came for the Tricycle. He got on it and pedalled out into the spring sunshine, ringing his bell loudly.

'Will it be our turn next?' asked Jumping Jack.

'Not yet,' said the Wheelbarrow.

Then a little girl, whose name was Cathy, came into the shed. 'Look, there's my ball!' she shouted, and hugged the Ball tightly. But it sagged and made a hissing noise because it had a split in its rubber tummy.

'Oh, you horrid Ball!' Cathy cried, and threw it back in the Wheelbarrow. Instead she took the Skipping Rope and ran out with it into the sunshine. She jumped and skipped so hard her hair stood out like a halo round her head.

'Why didn't she take the Ball with her?' asked Jumping Jack. But the Wheelbarrow only said 'Hmm.' It didn't want to be unkind to the poor Ball.

Nothing more was said. But a few days later they could hear a bouncing noise outside the shed; *bump-bump* it went against the wall, and the Wheelbarrow knew what that meant. So did the Old Ball; it lay there sighing through its crack all day long.

The Wheelbarrow thought about this for a long time —several days and nights. Then last night, after everyone had gone to bed, as I said, it gave a wooden creak and said to the Old Ball:

'I think it's a shame you're never to go out in the sunshine again. And I'm sorry to have to be the one to tell you, but you do understand, don't you, that Cathy has got a new ball and she's forgotten about you?'

'Yes,' sighed the Old Ball.

'I don't think Peter has forgotten *me*,' said Jumping Jack; 'he made such a fuss of me last summer. Anyway, it was just a mistake my being put out here in the shed. It was the charlady who carried all the summer toys out here when the snow came, and she didn't notice I'd got mixed up with them. I've been jumping mad ever since!'

'There's no need to get hoity-toity and stick your nose in the air even if you were only made last summer. You never know how long you will last. I've seen many jumping jacks in my time. They're fine as long as the strings don't break and both arms and legs are working. But sooner or later something gets broken and that's the end of that. . . . Well, not always, of course!' he added quickly when he saw that Jumping Jack looked quite frightened and ready to cry.

'I'm not at all perfect myself,' the Wheelbarrow went on. 'There's a weakness in one of my arms. The carpenter, who made me, put a thick layer of paint over the crack, so that it wouldn't show. But I've often been afraid when Peter filled me up with sand. Last year, I almost broke several times, so I don't think he'll use me again when summer comes along.'

'What a shame!' wheezed the Old Ball. He was sorry for the Wheelbarrow, but pleased at the same time that he wouldn't be left all alone in the dark shed.

'Then it's just me who is going out in the sunshine,' said Jumping Jack in a cheeky sort of way.

'You ought to be ashamed of yourself!' said the Wheelbarrow. 'We're all in the same boat—or rather, you and the Old Ball are in the same barrow, and that barrow happens to be me. And now I'm going to tell you what we're going to do—we three.'

'Do? What can we three do?' asked Jumping Jack.

'Listen. A long time ago there was an old wheelbarrow in here which told me that a night would come when all old broken or unwanted toys would come to life and go off and find new homes for themselves. I've been waiting for that night ever since, and now tonight I really think it's come, for I feel a sort of twitching and tingling in my wheel as if it wants to run. Yes, I'm sure we must be off!'

'But I don't want to go with you!' shouted Jumping Jack, 'I want to stay with Peter. I want to go back to the nursery with all the other toys; I don't want to go to a new home!'

But before he could say any more the Wheelbarrow

lifted his arms and rolled out of the shed with the Old Ball and Jumping Jack. The wheel creaked, the Old Ball sighed and Jumping Jack's arms and legs were tossing to and fro, so that it looked as if he was trying to get out, which, of course, was what he *wanted* to do. But the Wheelbarrow just went steadily on, balancing on one wheel.

Soon they met other toys; first a tricycle with crooked

handlebars which lurched from one side of the road to the other and nearly ran over them.

'Good evening,' said the Wheelbarrow.

'I think you should say "Good night" when it's so late,' said the Tricycle. 'I don't know why, but I had such an awful itch in my pedals, I just had to come out on to the road. And now I don't know where I'm going. . . .' And he was off, lurching from side to side.

After a while they met a doll with only one arm.

'Good night!' said the Wheelbarrow, for he was not going to make the same mistake twice.

'Good night!' said the Doll as she danced and pranced in her pink knitted slippers.

'Where are you going?' the Wheelbarrow called after her.

'I don't know. And I don't know where I come from. I just know I have to keep on and on!'

'Why couldn't she have come with us?' asked Jumping Jack, when she had disappeared.

'Stupid!' said the Barrow. 'Don't you understand that the whole idea is that each toy should go to a different home? If one child gets a whole lot of old broken toys the same thing will happen again—some of them will be thrown away. No, each child is to have *one* toy.' And they rolled on.

They met many queer toys.

A skipping rope came waving along the road, and after it a humming-top, tripping and bumping over the stones in the road. A very small toy train came chuffing along at full speed. It headed straight for the ditch and disappeared under the water. But a moment later—*bubble-bubble, bubble-bubble, whoosh!*—up it came on the other side and ran straight into a wooden hoop which was bowling in the opposite direction. The hoop fell over, the train fell over, but that didn't worry them; they were up and off again before you could count three. A teddy-bear with a split down the back came plodding by. All he needed was a bit more sawdust stuffing and a few stitches, and some little girl would be glad to have him and mend his back.

After a time the Old Ball started rolling about in the barrow in a restless sort of way: 'I say, Wheelbarrow, can you stop a minute? There's a little cottage up there by the wood; something tells me I have to get off here.'

The Wheelbarrow stopped to let the Old Ball roll off, and it bounced up on the cottage window to look in. Sure enough there was a little girl asleep in bed clutching an old rag doll.

'This must be the place all right,' said the Old Ball. 'Thanks for bringing me along and for being so kind to me. I'll just stay here on the doorstep, then she's sure to find me in the morning. Goodbye!'

The Wheelbarrow and Jumping Jack said goodbye and rolled on until the Barrow suddenly said, 'I can feel a sort of pull inside me; I think we have to turn up this little path through the wood.'

So they did. There was still a bit of snow here and there, making the wheel go *crunch, crunch.*

At last they came to a clearing with an even smaller

cottage than the one where the Old Ball had stopped. The snow lay in drifts against the windows, so the Wheelbarrow took a run at one of them and managed to get high enough to look in. And there was a little boy asleep. By the stove stood a box with a string tied to it. That was all *he* had in the way of a wheelbarrow.

'There, I *thought* so!' said the Wheelbarrow. 'This is the place for me. But what about you, Jack? Haven't *you* felt anything yet? Haven't you had an itch in those long arms and legs of yours as if somebody was pulling your string?'

'No, I haven't!' said Jumping Jack very crossly. 'I'm

not broken, that's why. It's only the broken and cast-off toys who have to find new homes; I have Peter to love me at home, and I don't know why you brought me along—especially when I shouted to you to let me off, you stupid old bundle of sticks!'

'It wasn't my fault. Just when you wanted to get out, something told me to start off and take you with me, so I did.'

Then suddenly the Barrow *knew* why he had brought Jack along. 'Don't you understand? You had to see for yourself what happens tonight, so that you can go home and tell all the other toys. You must tell them they needn't worry even if they do get broken. There are lots of children who will have them and mend them too, so that they're as good as new.'

And all at once Jumping Jack could see it too. 'You're quite right,' he said.

And then he found, to his surprise, that he could move. What fun it was to stretch his legs and arms without being jerked by the string! He hopped first on one leg, then the other, and then he turned complete somersaults. Then he thanked the Wheelbarrow for his trip and said goodbye.

After that, with his string floating straight out behind him like a tail, he ran and ran till he reached the little shed in the garden at home.

And now Jumping Jack has been waiting all day for it to grow dark; for not until the children are in bed and asleep can he go out and give his message to all the broken and unwanted toys.

* * * * *

So if you wake up tomorrow morning and find that your old doll seems to be smiling just a little, or that your chipped trumpet sounds better than it has for a long time, that will be because Jumping Jack has told them about the trip he made with his friends the Wheelbarrow and the Old Ball last night.

The potato with big ideas

THERE was once a potato which lay waiting for someone to come and dig it up. The other potatoes were just

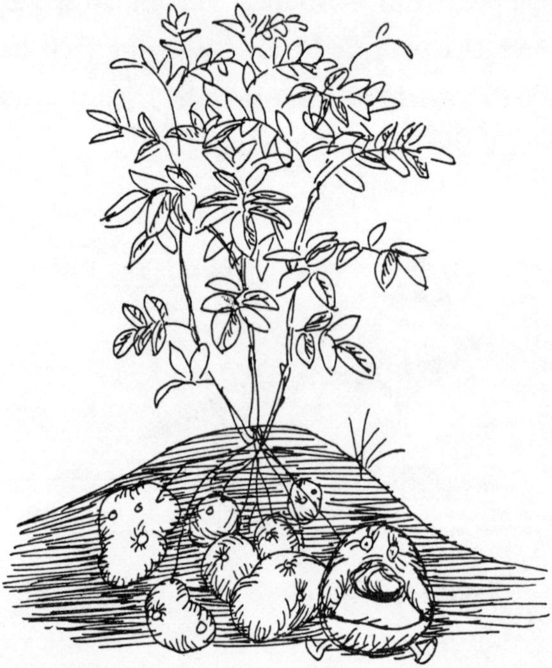

quietly growing larger and larger, but this particular potato had ideas; he was stuck-up. And he was bored with waiting.

'Hi, everybody!' the stuck-up potato said. 'I'm not

going to wait any longer. I'll try to get out of this hole by myself. People must be longing to see what a beautiful potato I am; everything that is beautiful must see the light of day and enjoy the sunshine. Here I come! The most beautiful potato in all the world!'

You may know that all potatoes are tied to the mother potato by a thin thread (so that she can keep them in order, no doubt). Now that stuck-up potato began tugging at his thread, and the thread stretched and stretched till one fine day the stuck-up potato found himself lying on the ground above.

'Hurrah, hurrah! Here I am at last! Good morning, Mr. Weed! Good morning, Mrs. Worm! I am the world's most beautiful potato. And if you, Mr. Sun, would like to shine on me for a moment, you can.'

'With the greatest of pleasure,' answered the sun, 'but it won't be good for you, you know.'

'Who cares? You just shine away and let me enjoy a nice hot sun-bath.'

So the sun shone on that stuck-up potato and turned him blue, green, red and purple all over. This made the potato more pleased with himself than ever:

'When the boys come past and see me lying here they will say: "My goodness! What a fine potato! We must take that home to Mother for dinner." And one of them will put me carefully in his pocket. When his mother sees me she will say: "Goodness gracious! What a wonderful potato; it's much too good for me. I will give it to the parson." And when the parson sees me he will say: "Goodness gracious! My, oh my! What a marvellous potato; I'll give it to the bishop." And when the bishop sees me he will say: "Goodness gracious! My, oh my! And bless my soul! But what an exquisite potato. I must send it straight to the Pope in Rome." Then I will be wrapped in silver paper and sent to the Pope. And when the Pope sees me he will put on his finest clothes and sit on his best silver throne and put me on a gold plate and eat me, while all the church bells ring to tell the world that now the Pope is eating the most beautiful potato from Puddlington-on-the-Marsh.'

But just as the potato was having this lovely dream, the farmer and his wife and their little boy came out into the field to start lifting the potatoes.

They sang as they worked, and shouted to each other every time they found a really whacking big potato.

'Wait till they see *me*, then they'll have something to crow about!' thought the stuck-up potato.

Suddenly the little boy shouted: 'Look at this funny-looking potato! It's blue and red and green all over!'

'Throw it in the pig-bucket,' said his father; 'you can't eat that sort. It's been on top of the earth instead of underneath, where it should have been. But the pigs won't mind what colour it is.'

And so that stuck-up potato ended his days in the pig-trough instead of on a gold plate in the Pope's palace in Rome, which all goes to show that even if you have big ideas it's sometimes wiser to leave them alone.

The mice and the Christmas tree

Now you shall hear the story about a family of mice who lived behind the larder wall.

* * * * *

Every Christmas Eve, Mother Mouse and the children swept and dusted their whole house with their tails, and for a Christmas tree Father Mouse decorated an old boot with spider's web instead of tinsel. For Christmas presents, the children were each given a little nut, and Mother Mouse held up a piece of bacon fat for them all to sniff.

After that, they danced round and round the boot, and sang and played games till they were tired out. Then

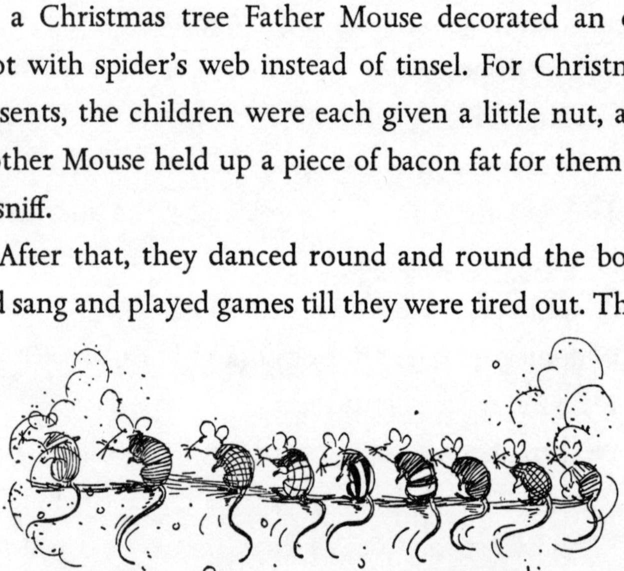

Father Mouse would say: 'That's all for tonight! Time to go to bed!'

That is how it had been every Christmas and that is how it was to be this year. The little mice held each other by the tail and danced round the boot, while Granny Mouse enjoyed the fun from her rocking-chair, which wasn't a rocking-chair at all, but a small turnip.

But when Father Mouse said, 'That's all for tonight! Time to go to bed!' all the children dropped each other's tails and shouted: 'No! No!'

'What's that?' said Father Mouse. 'When I say it's time for bed, it's time for bed!'

'We don't want to go!' cried the children, and hid behind Granny's turnip rocking-chair.

'What's all this nonsense?' said Mother Mouse. 'Christmas is over now, so off you go, the lot of you!'

'No, no!' wailed the children, and climbed on to Granny's knee. She hugged them all lovingly. 'Why don't you want to go to bed, my little sugar lumps?'

'Because we want to go upstairs to the big drawing-

room and dance round a proper Christmas tree,' said the eldest Mouse child. 'You see, I've been peeping through a crack in the wall and I saw a huge Christmas tree with lots and lots of lights on it.'

'We want to see the Christmas tree and all the lights too!' shouted the other children.

'Oh, but the drawing-room can be a very dangerous place for mice,' said Granny.

'Not when all the people have gone to bed,' objected the eldest Mouse child.

'Oh, do let's go!' they all pleaded.

Mother and Father Mouse didn't know what to say, but they couldn't very well disappoint the children on Christmas Eve.

'Perhaps we could take them up there just for a minute or two,' suggested Mother Mouse.

'Very well,' said Father, 'but follow me closely.'

So they set off. They tiptoed past three tins of herring, two large jars of honey and a barrel of cider.

'We have to go very carefully here,' whispered Father Mouse, 'not to knock over any bottles. Are you all right, Granny?'

'Of course I'm all right,' said Granny, 'you just carry on. I haven't been up in the drawing-room since I was a little Mouse girl; it'll be fun to see it all again.'

'Mind the trap!' said the eldest Mouse child. 'It's behind that sack of potatoes.'

'I know that,' said Granny; 'it's been there since I was

a child. I'm not afraid of that!' And she took a flying leap right over the trap and scuttled after the others up the wall.

'What a lovely tree!' cried all the children when they peeped out of the hole by the drawing-room fireplace. 'But where are the lights? You said there'd be lots and lots of lights, didn't you? Didn't you?' The children shouted, crowding round the eldest one, who was quite sure there had been lights the day before.

They stood looking for a little while. Then suddenly a whole lot of coloured lights lit up the tree! Do you know what had happened? By accident, Granny had touched the electric switch by the fireplace.

'Oh, how lovely!' they all exclaimed, and Father and Mother and Granny thought it was very nice too. They walked right round the tree, looking at the decorations, the little paper baskets, the glass balls and the glittering tinsel garlands. But the children found something even more exciting: a mechanical lorry!

Of course, they couldn't wind it up themselves, but its young master had wound it up before he went to bed, to be ready for him to play with in the morning. So when the Mouse children clambered into it, it started off right away.

'Children, children! You mustn't make such a noise!' warned Mother Mouse.

But the children didn't listen; they were having a wonderful time going round and round and round in the lorry.

'As long as the cat doesn't come!' said Father Mouse anxiously.

He had hardly spoken before the cat walked silently through the open door.

Father, Mother and Granny Mouse all made a dash for the hole in the skirting but the children were trapped in the lorry, which just went on going round and round and round. They had never been so scared in all their Mouse lives.

The cat crouched under the tree, and every time the lorry passed she tried to tap it with her front paw. But it was going too fast and she missed.

Then the lorry started slowing down. 'I think we'd better make a jump for it and try to get up in the tree,' said the eldest Mouse. So when the lorry stopped they all gave a big jump and landed on the branches of the tree.

One hid in a paper basket, another behind a bulb (which nearly burned him), a third swung on a glass ball and the fourth rolled himself up in some cotton wool. But where was the eldest Mouse? Oh yes, he had climbed right to the top and was balancing next to the star and shouting at the cat:

'Silly, silly cat,
You can't catch us!
You're much too fat,
Silly, silly cat!'

But the cat pretended not to hear or see the little mice. She sharpened her claws on the lorry. 'I'm not interested in catching mice tonight,' she said as if to herself, 'I've been waiting for a chance to play with this lorry all day.'

'Pooh! That's just a story!' said the eldest who was also the bravest. 'You'd catch us quick enough if we came down.'

'No, I wouldn't. Not on Christmas Eve!' said the cat. And she kept her word. When they did all come timidly down, she never moved, but just said: 'Hurry back to your hole, children. Christmas Eve is the one night when I'm kind to little mice. But woe betide you if I catch you tomorrow morning!'

The little mice pelted through that hole and never stopped running till they got to their home behind the larder wall. There were Father and Mother and Granny Mouse waiting in fear and trembling to know what had happened to them.

When Mother Mouse had heard their story she said, 'You must promise me, children, never to go up to the drawing-room again.'

'We promise! We promise!' they all shouted together. Then she made them say after her *The Mouse Law*, which they'd all been taught when they were tiny:

'We promise always to obey
Our parents dear in every way,
To wipe our feet upon the mat
And never, never cheek the cat.

Remember too the awful danger
Of taking money from a stranger;
We will not go off on our own
Or give our mother cause to moan.

Odd bits of cheese and bacon-scraps
Are almost certain to be traps,
So we must look for bigger things
Like loaves and cakes and doughnut-rings;

And if these rules we still obey
We'll live to run another day.'

Never take no for an answer

YOU see the old woman spinning yarn? She was hard at work one day when a young mouse came out of the hole by the stove.

'Well, well, fancy seeing you,' said the old woman.

'Peep, peep!' said the little mouse. 'My ma sent me to ask what the yarn is for that you're spinning?'

'It's for a jersey for my husband; the one he has is so worn he can't use it any more,' answered the old woman.

'Peep, peep! I'd better go and tell that to my ma!' And the little mouse disappeared down the hole. The old woman went on spinning, but it wasn't long before she heard a scuffling by the stove and there sat the mouse once more.

'You back again?' she asked.

'Peep, peep! My ma said to ask you who is to have your husband's old jersey when he gets the new one?'

'I'm going to use that myself when I milk the cows, because my old milking jacket isn't fit to wear any more,' said the old woman.

'Peep, peep! I'd better go and tell that to my ma,' said the mouse, and he was gone. But in no time at all he was back again.

'What d'you want to know this time?' the old woman asked.

'Peep, peep! My ma wants to know who is to have your old milking jacket when you get your husband's old jersey and he gets the new one?'

'The dog is going to have it in his kennel, because his old rug is so thin it's no good any more.'

'Peep, peep! I'd better go and tell that to my ma,' said the little mouse, and darted away to his hole by the stove. But he had hardly popped in before he popped out again.

'That was quick!' said the woman. 'What is it now?'

'Peep, peep! My ma wants to know who is to have the dog's old rug when he gets your old milking jacket and you get your husband's old jersey and he gets the new one?' said the mouse all in one breath.

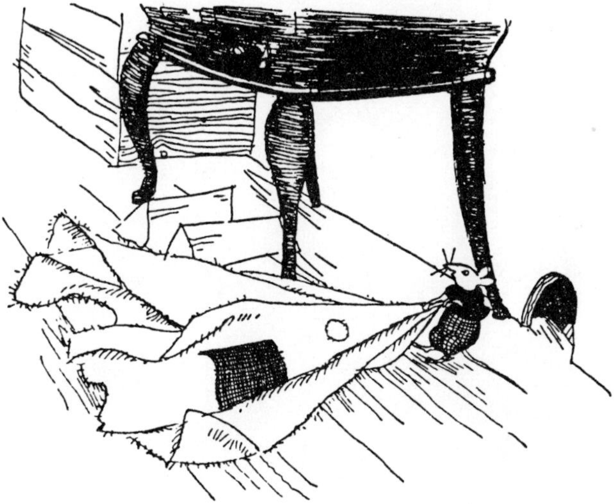

'You can have it, if you like,' said the old woman.

'Peep, peep! Thank you *very* much,' said the little mouse. 'Now there'll be an eiderdown for *our* bed as well!' And he was so pleased he sang this song:

'Oh me, oh my!
We'll soon be as snug
As a bug in a rug,
What do you think of that!
Come and see me any time
I'll make you up another rhyme,
But please don't bring the cat.'

Mr. Learn-a-lot and the singing midges

ONE warm summer night Mrs. Midge said to her daughters, 'We'll go and visit Mr. Learn-a-lot, the schoolmaster.'

'What do we want to do that for?' asked the young midges. There were three of them: Big Sister Midge, Middle Sister Midge and Wee Sister Midge.

'We're going to sing to him. You're all so good at singing now, it's a pleasure to listen to you, and Mr. Learn-a-lot is such a good judge of music.'

So they all flew off to Mr. Learn-a-lot's house and hovered outside his bedroom window. Mrs. Midge peered through the glass while her daughters all talked at once in high, squeaky voices:

'Is the window shut, Mama?'

'Won't he open it, Mama?'

'Can't we get in, Mama?'

'I expect he'll open the window when he goes to bed,' said Mrs. Midge.

'He's opening the window now, Mama!'

'Can we go in now, Mama?'

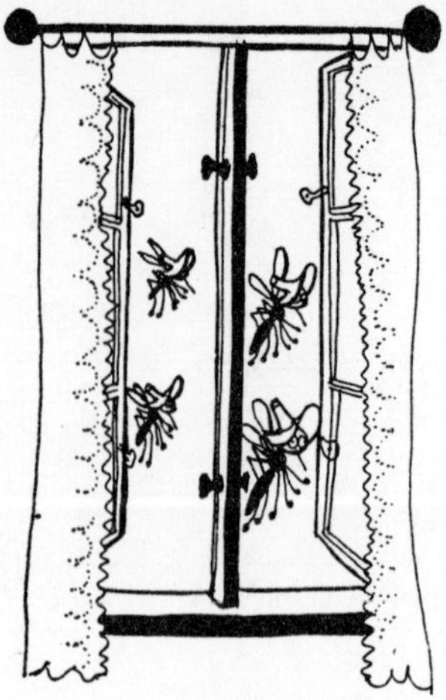

'What shall we sing for him, Mama?'

'Not so fast, children, there's no hurry. Let Mr. Learn-a-lot get nicely into bed first.'

'He's climbing into bed now, Mama! He's in bed, really he is, Mama! Wouldn't it be dreadful if he fell asleep before he heard our singing, Mama?' squeaked all the little midges. But Mrs. Midge was sure the schoolmaster would wake up again when they started singing.

'I think Big Sister Midge had better go in first,' she said.

'All right, but what am I to sing, Mama?'

'You can sing the song about "We midges have not got . . .",' said Mrs. Midge, and settled herself with her two younger daughters behind the curtain. 'And remember to fly in a circle over his head. If he likes your song he will sit up in bed. Now off you go!'

And Big Sister Midge flew round and round in a circle over Mr. Learn-a-lot's head and sang this song:

'We midges have not got a couple of beans
Yet in summer we all are as happy as queens,
For every night in a swoon of delight
We dance to the tune of our dizzy flight,
And all we need to keep in the pink
Is a tiny drop of your blood to drink.'

Three times she sang the same verse, and she was beginning to think Mr. Learn-a-lot didn't care for her song at all. But suddenly he sat bolt upright in bed.

'Come back! Come back, child!' whispered Mrs. Midge.

'Was I all right, Mama?'

'You were very good. Now we'll just wait till Mr. Learn-a-lot has fallen asleep again, then it'll be Middle Sister's turn. You can sing the song about "How doth the little busy me"—that is so very funny! There! Now I think it would be all right for you to start. But you mustn't leave off before Mr. Learn-a-lot has got right out of bed and is standing in the middle of the floor. Fly a little higher than your sister did. Off you go!'

And Middle Sister Midge sang as loudly as she could while she flew round and round the schoolmaster's head:

'How doth the little busy me
Improve each shady hour
By settling on your nose or knee
As if upon a flower.'

She hadn't sung more than one verse before Mr. Learn-a-lot threw off the bedclothes and tumbled out of bed.

'Come back, come back!' whispered Mrs. Midge.

'Wasn't I good?' said Middle Sister as she arrived back all out of breath. 'And I wasn't a bit afraid of him!'

'That'll do; we midges are not in the habit of boasting,' said Mrs. Midge. 'Now it's Wee Sister's turn.'

'What shall I sing?' asked the smallest midge with the tiniest voice you ever heard.

'You can sing our evening song—you know—the one that goes:

'The day is done and all rejoice
To hear again this still small voice.
May the music of my wings
Console you for my little stings.'

That's just the thing for tonight,' Mrs. Midge added thoughtfully.

'Oh yes, I know that one,' said Wee Sister; she was very pleased her mother had chosen one she knew.

'I expect it will be the last song tonight,' said Mrs. Midge, 'and don't worry if you don't get right through it. If Mr. Learn-a-lot suddenly claps his hands you must be sure to come back to me at once. Will you remember that?'

'Yes, Mama,' said Wee Sister, and off she flew.

Mr. Learn-a-lot was lying absolutely still. So Wee Sister began to sing—all on one top note:

'The day is done——'

Smack! Mr. Learn-a-lot clapped his hands together.

'Come back, come back!' called Mrs. Midge. But there was no sign of Wee Sister.

'Oh, my darling, sweet wee one, please come back to your mother!' wailed Mrs. Midge. No sound—no sound at all for a long time; then suddenly Wee Sister was sitting on the curtain beside them.

'Didn't you hear me calling?' asked Mrs. Midge very sternly.

'Oh yes, but you said I was to fly very, very quietly, and that clap of Mr. Learn-a-lot's sent me flying right into the darkest corner of the room.'

'Poor darling!' said Mrs. Midge. 'But you're safe back now. You've all been very good and very clever girls. And now I'd like to hear what you think of Mr. Learn-a-lot?'

Big Sister answered, 'He's nice; he likes the one who sings longest best!'

Middle Sister answered, 'He's very polite; he gets out of bed for the one who sings loudest!'

And Wee Sister said, 'I think he's very musical; he claps the one with the sweetest voice!'

'Yes, yes, that's all very true,' said Mrs. Midge; 'but now I will tell you something else about Mr. Learn-a-lot. He is not only a very learned gentleman, but he will provide us with the nicest, most enjoyable supper, and we needn't even wake him up. Shall we go?'

'Oh, that is a fine idea!' cried Big Sister, Middle Sister and Wee Sister Midge, for they always did just what their mother told them.

Poor Mr. Learn-a-lot!

Mrs Pepperpot Again
and other stories

MRS PEPPERPOT AGAIN

and other stories by

ALF PRØYSEN

Translated by Marianne Helweg

Illustrated by

BJÖRN BERG

Contents

Mrs. Pepperpot tries to please her husband

THINGS were not very lively at Mrs. Pepperpot's house. Mr. Pepperpot was in a bad mood—he had been in it for days—and Mrs. Pepperpot simply didn't know how to get him out of it. She put flowers on the table and cooked him his favourite dish, fried bacon with macaroni cheese. But it was all no use; Mr. Pepperpot just went on moping.

'I don't know what's the matter with him,' sighed Mrs. Pepperpot, 'perhaps he's pining for pancakes.' So she made him a big pile of pancakes.

When her husband came in for dinner his face lit up at the sight of them, but as soon as he'd sat down and picked up his knife and fork to start eating, his face fell again; he was as glum as before.

'Ah well!' he said, staring up at the ceiling, 'I suppose it's too much to expect.'

'I've had enough of this!' cried Mrs. Pepperpot. 'You tell me what's wrong, or I'll *shrink*, so I will!' (You remember that Mrs. Pepperpot had a habit of shrinking to the size of a pepperpot, though not usually, I'm afraid, when she *wanted* to, but at the most inconvenient moments.) 'You have something on your mind, that's quite clear,' she went on. 'But you don't think of me, do you? Watching your face getting longer every day is no joke, I can tell you. Now even pancakes can't cheer you up.'

'Pancakes are all right,' nodded Mr. Pepperpot, 'but there's something else missing.'

'What could that be?' asked his wife.

'Couldn't we sometimes have a bit of bilberry jam with the pancakes, instead of just eating them plain?' And Mr. Pepperpot gave a great sigh.

At last she understood; it *was* a very long time since she had given him bilberry jam, and that was what the poor man had been missing.

'Well, if that's all you want, I'll go and pick some bilberries this very minute,' said Mrs. Pepperpot, and she snatched a bucket from a hook on the wall and rushed out of the door.

She walked rather fast because she was cross with her husband, and as she walked she talked to herself: 'I've got the silliest husband alive,' she muttered. 'I was a fool to marry him. In fact, there's only one bigger fool than me, and that's him. *Oh*, how stupid he is!'

In no time at all she reached the spot in the forest where the bilberries grew. She put her bucket under a bush and started picking into the cup she had in her apron pocket. Every time the cup was full she emptied it into the bucket. Cup after cup went in, until the bucket needed only one more cup to be quite full. But then, just as she had picked the last bilberry into the cup, lo and behold! She shrank to the size of a pepperpot.

'Now we're in a jam, that's certain, and I don't mean bilberry jam!' said the little old woman, who now had a tiny voice like a mouse. 'Still, I expect I can manage to get the cup as far as the bucket if I push and pull hard enough. After that we'll have to think again.'

So she crooked her arm through the handle and dragged the cup along. It was very hard at first, but then she came to an ant-path made of slippery pine-needles; here it was much easier, because the cup could slide along it. And all the time little ants and big ants kept scuttling to and fro beside her. She tried to talk to them.

'How d'you do, ants,' she said. 'Hard at work, I see. Yes, there's always plenty to do and that's a fact.' But the ants were far too busy to answer.

'Couldn't you stop for a minute and talk to me?' she asked. But they just hurried on. 'Well, I shall have to talk to myself; then I won't be disturbing anybody.' And she sat down with her back leaning against the cup.

As she sat there, she suddenly felt something breathe down her neck; she turned round, and saw a fox standing there waving his tail in a friendly sort of way.

'Hullo, Mr. Fox. Are you out for a stroll?' said Mrs. Pepperpot. 'Lucky you don't know my hens are . . . Oh dear! I nearly let my tongue run away with me!'

'Where did you say your hens were, Mrs. Pepperpot?' asked the fox in his silkiest voice.

'That would be telling, wouldn't it?' said Mrs. Pepperpot. 'But, as you see, I'm rather busy just now; I've got to get this cup of bilberries hauled over to the bucket somehow, so I haven't time to talk to you.'

'I'll carry the cup for you,' said the fox, as polite as could be. 'Then you can talk while we walk.'

'Thanks very much,' said Mrs. Pepperpot. 'As I was saying, my hens are . . . There now! I nearly said it again!'

The fox smiled encouragingly: 'Just go on talking, it doesn't matter what you say to *me*.'

'I'm not usually one to gossip, but somehow it seems so easy to talk about my hens being . . . Goodness, why don't I keep my mouth shut? Anyway, there's the bucket. So, if you would be so kind and set the cup down beside it I'll tell you where my hens are.'

'That's right, you tell me. Your hens will be quite safe with me.'

'They certainly will!' laughed Mrs. Pepperpot, 'for they're all away! They were broody, so I lent them to the neighbours to hatch out their eggs.'

Then the fox saw he had been tricked, and he was so ashamed he slunk away into the forest and hid himself.

'Ha, ha, ha! That was a fine trick you played on the fox!' said a voice quite close to Mrs. Pepperpot. She looked up and there stood a wolf towering over her.

'Well, if it isn't Mr. Wolf!' said Mrs. Pepperpot, swallowing hard to keep up her courage. 'The ve . . very person I need. You can help me tip this cup of bilberries into the bucket.'

'Oh no, you can't fool me like you did the fox,' said the wolf.

'I'm not trying to fool you at all,' said Mrs. Pepperpot; she had had a good idea and was no longer afraid. 'You'd better do as I say or I'll send for One-eye Threadless!'

The wolf laughed. 'I've heard many old wives' tales but I've never heard that one before!'

'It's not an old wives' tale,' said Mrs. Pepperpot indignantly, 'and I'm not just an old wife; I'm Mrs. Pepperpot who can shrink and grow again all in a flash. One-eye Threadless is my servant.'

'Ha, ha! I'd like to see that servant of yours!' laughed the wolf.

'Very well; stick your nose into my apron pocket here and you'll meet him,' said Mrs. Pepperpot. So the wolf put his nose in her apron pocket and pricked it very severely on a needle she kept there.

'Ow, ow!' he shouted and started running towards the forest. But Mrs. Pepperpot called him back at once: 'Come here! You haven't done your job yet; empty that cup into that bucket, and don't you dare spill a single berry, or I'll send for One-eye Threadless to prick you again!'

The wolf didn't dare disobey her, but as soon as he had emptied the cup into the bucket he ran like the fox to the forest to hide.

Mrs. Pepperpot had a good laugh as she watched him go, but then she heard something rustle near the bucket. This time it was the big brown bear himself.

'Dear me! What an honour!' said Mrs. Pepperpot in a shaky voice, and she curtsied so low she nearly disappeared in the bushes. 'Has the fine weather tempted Your Majesty out for a walk?'

'Yes,' growled the big brown bear and went on sniffing at the bucket.

'How very fortunate for me! As Your Majesty can see, I've picked a whole bucket of berries, but it's not very safe for a little old woman like myself to walk in the forest alone. Could I ask Your Majesty to carry the bucket out to the road for me?'

'I don't know about that,' said the bear. 'I like bilberries myself.'

'Yes, of course, but you're not like the rest of them,

Your Majesty; you wouldn't rob a poor little old woman like me!'

'Bilberries; that's what I want!' said the bear, and put his head down to start eating.

In a flash Mrs. Pepperpot had jumped on his neck and started tickling him behind his ears.

'What are you doing?' asked the bear.

'I'm just tickling your ears for you,' answered Mrs. Pepperpot. 'Doesn't it feel good?'

'Good? It's almost better than eating the berries!' said the bear.

'Well, if Your Majesty would be so kind as to carry the bucket, I could be tickling Your Majesty's ears all the way,' said the artful Mrs. Pepperpot.

'Oh, very well then,' grumbled the bear.

When they reached the road the bear put the bucket down very carefully on a flat stone.

'Many, many thanks, Your Majesty,' said Mrs. Pepperpot as she made another deep curtsey.

'Thank *you*,' said the bear, and shuffled off into the forest.

When the bear had gone Mrs. Pepperpot became her usual size again, so she picked up her bucket and hurried homeward.

'It's really not very difficult to look after yourself, even when you're only the size of a pepperpot,' she told herself. 'As long as you know how to tackle the people you meet. Cunning people must be tricked, cowardly ones must be frightened, and the big, strong ones must have their ears tickled.'

As for bad-tempered husbands, the only thing to do with *them* is to give them bilberry jam with their pancakes.

Mrs. Pepperpot minds the baby

Now I'll tell you what happened the day Mrs. Pepperpot was asked to mind the baby.

It was early in the morning. Mrs. Pepperpot had sent her husband off to work. In the usual way wives do, she had made the coffee and the sandwiches for his lunch, and had stood by the window and waved till he was out of sight. Then, just like other wives, she had gone back to bed to have a little extra shut-eye, leaving all her housework for later.

She had been sleeping a couple of hours when there was a knock at the door. She looked at the clock. 'Good heavens!' she cried, 'have I slept so long?' She pulled her clothes on very quickly and ran to open the door.

In the porch stood a lady with a little boy on her arm.

'Forgive me for knocking,' said the lady.

'You're welcome,' said Mrs. Pepperpot.

'You see,' said the lady, 'I'm staying with my aunt near here with my little boy, and today we simply *have* to go shopping in the town. I can't take Roger and there's no one in the house to look after him.'

'Oh, that's all right!' said Mrs. Pepperpot. 'I'll look after your little boy.' (To herself she thought: 'However will I manage with all that work and me oversleeping like that. Ah well, I shall have to do both at the same time.') Then she said out loud: 'Roger, come to Mrs. Pepperpot? That's right!' And she took the baby from the lady.

'You don't need to give him a meal,' said the lady. 'I've brought some apples he can have when he starts sucking his fingers.'

'Very well,' said Mrs. Pepperpot, and put the apples in a dish on the sideboard.

The lady said goodbye and Mrs. Pepperpot set the baby down on the rug in the sitting-room. Then she went out into the kitchen to fetch her broom to start sweeping up. At that very moment she *shrank*!

'Oh dear! Oh dear! Whatever shall I do?' she wailed, for of course now she was much smaller than the baby. She gave up any idea of cleaning the house; when her husband came home she would have to tell him that she had had a headache.

'I must go and see what that little fellow is doing,' she thought, as she climbed over the doorstep into the sitting-room. Not a moment too soon! For Roger had crawled right across the floor and was just about to pull the tablecloth off the table together with a pot of jam, a loaf of bread, and a big jug of coffee!

Mrs. Pepperpot lost no time. She knew it was too far for her to get to the table, so she pushed over a large silver cup which was standing on the floor, waiting to be polished. Her husband had won it in a skiing competition years ago when he was young.

The cup made a fine booming noise as it fell; the baby turned round and started crawling towards it.

'That's right,' said Mrs. Pepperpot, 'you play with that; at least you can't break it.'

But Roger wasn't after the silver cup. Gurgling: 'Ha' dolly! Ha' dolly!' he made a bee-line for Mrs. Pepperpot, and before she could get away, he had grabbed her by the waist! He jogged her up and down and every time Mrs. Pepperpot kicked and wriggled to get free, he laughed. ''Ickle, 'ickle!' he shouted, for she was tickling his hand with her feet.

'Let go! Let go!' yelled Mrs. Pepperpot. But Roger was used to his father shouting 'Let's go!' when he threw him up in the air and caught him again. So Roger shouted 'Leggo! Leggo!' and threw the little old woman up in the air with all the strength of his short arms. Mrs. Pepperpot went up and up—nearly to the ceiling! Luckily she landed on the sofa, but she bounced several times before she could stop.

'Talk of flying through the air with the greatest of ease!' she gasped. 'If that had happened to me in my normal size I'd most likely have broken every bone in my body. Ah well, I'd better see what my little friend is up to now.'

She soon found out. Roger had got hold of a match-box and was trying to strike a match. Luckily he was using the wrong side of the box, but Mrs. Pepperpot had to think very quickly indeed.

'Youngsters like to copy everything you do, so I'll take this nut and throw it at him. Then he'll throw it at me—I hope.'

She had found the nut in the sofa and now she was in such a hurry to throw it she forgot to aim properly. But it was a lucky shot and it hit Roger just behind the ear, making him turn round. 'What else can I throw?' wondered Mrs. Pepperpot, but there was no need, because the baby had seen her; he dropped the match-box and started crawling towards the sofa.

'Ha' dolly! Ha' dolly!' he gurgled delightedly. And now they started a very funny game of hide-and-seek—at least it was fun for Roger, but not quite so amusing for poor little old Mrs. Pepperpot who had to hide behind the cushions to get away from him. In the end she managed to climb on to the sideboard where she kept a precious geranium in a pot.

'Aha, you can't catch me now!' she said, feeling much safer.

But at that moment the baby decided to go back to the match-box. 'No, no, no!' shouted Mrs. Pepperpot. Roger took no notice. So, when she saw he was trying to strike another match, she put her back against the flowerpot and gave it a push so that it fell to the floor with a crash.

Roger immediately left the match-box for this new and interesting mess of earth and bits of broken flowerpot. He buried both his hands in it and started putting it in his mouth, gurgling, 'Nice din-din!'

'No, no, no!' shouted Mrs. Pepperpot once more. 'Oh, whatever shall I do?' Her eye caught the apples left by Roger's mother. They were right beside her on the dish. One after the other she rolled them over the edge of the dish on to the floor. Roger watched them roll, then he decided to chase them, forgetting his lovely meal of earth and broken flowerpot. Soon the apples were all over the floor and the baby was crawling happily from one to the other.

There was a knock on the door.

'Come in,' said Mrs. Pepperpot.

Roger's mother opened the door and came in, and there was Mrs. Pepperpot as large as life, carrying a dust-pan full of earth and broken bits in one hand and her broom in the other.

'Has he been naughty?' asked the lady.

'As good as gold,' said Mrs. Pepperpot. 'We've had a high old time together, haven't we, Roger?' And she handed him back to his mother.

'I'll have to take you home now, precious,' said the lady.

But the little fellow began to cry. 'Ha' dolly! Ha' dolly!' he sobbed.

'Have *dolly*?' said his mother. 'But you didn't bring a dolly—you don't even have one at home.' She turned to Mrs. Pepperpot. 'I don't know what he means.'

'Oh, children say so many things grown-ups don't understand,' said Mrs. Pepperpot, and waved goodbye to Roger and his mother.

Then she set about cleaning up her house.

Mrs. Pepperpot's penny watchman

STRANGE things had been happening in Mrs. Pepperpot's house. It all began when a little girl came to the door selling penny raffle tickets for a tablecloth. Mrs. Pepperpot hunted high and low until she found a penny; it was a nice shiny one, because someone had been polishing it. But just as she was writing her name on the ticket, the penny dropped on the floor and rolled into a crack by the trapdoor to the cellar.

'Bang goes my fortune,' said Mrs. Pepperpot, as she watched it disappear. 'Now I won't be able to buy a raffle ticket after all. But I can't let you go without giving you anything; what about a nice home-made short-cake?' And she stood on a stool to reach the cake-tin.

It was empty. Mrs. Pepperpot turned the tin almost inside out, but there was no sign of any short-cake.

'I can't understand it,' she said. 'I baked two whole rounds of short-cake on Friday. Today it's only Monday, and the tin is empty. Very mysterious. But I've got something you might like even better, little girl.' So

saying, Mrs. Pepperpot opened the trapdoor to the cellar and went down the steps to fetch the big jar of bramble jelly she had left over from the summer.

But what a sight met her eyes!

'Goodness Gracious and Glory Be!' she exclaimed, for the big jar of bramble jelly was lying smashed under the shelf with the jelly gently oozing out over the floor. From the sticky mess a little trail of mouse footprints ran across to the chimney.

There was nothing for it—Mrs. Pepperpot had to go up to the little girl and tell her she couldn't even have bramble jelly. But the little girl said it didn't matter a bit and politely curtsied before going on to the next house.

Mrs. Pepperpot took a mouse-trap and went down the cellar steps again. She baited it with cheese and set it very carefully on the floor. When it was done she turned to go upstairs again, but the hem of her skirt brushed against it, and SNAP! went the trap, with a corner of her skirt caught in it. That was bad enough, but then, if you please, she shrank again!

'Now I really *am* stuck!' she told herself, and she certainly was; she couldn't move an inch. After she had sat there a while she saw a young mouse peeping over the edge of an empty flowerpot.

'You're quite safe to come out,' said Mrs. Pepperpot. 'I'm too well tethered to do you any harm at the moment.'

But the little mouse darted off to an empty cardboard box and then two little mice popped their noses over the edge.

'One and one makes two,' said Mrs. Pepperpot. 'I learned that at school, and I wouldn't be a bit surprised if you fetched a third one—for one and two make three!'

She was right. The two little mice darted off together and stayed away quite a long time while she sat and waited. Suddenly she heard a tinny little sound. Ping! Ping! And a big mouse came walking towards her on his hind legs, banging a shiny gong with a little steel pin. The shiny gong was Mrs. Pepperpot's lost penny!

The big mouse bowed low. 'Queen of the House, I greet you!' The little mice were peeping out from behind him.

'Thank goodness for that!' said Mrs. Pepperpot. 'For a moment I thought you might be coming to gobble me up—you're so much bigger than I am!'

'We're not in the habit of gobbling up queens,' said the large mouse. 'I just wanted to tell you, you have a thief in your house.'

Mrs. Pepperpot snorted. 'Thief indeed! Of course I have; you and all the other mice are the thieves in my house. Whose penny is it you're using for a gong, may I ask?'

'Oh, is that what it is? A penny?' said the big mouse. 'Well, it rolled through a crack in the floor, you see, so I thought I could use it to scare away the thief and to show I'm the watchman in this house. You really do need a watchman, Queen of the House, to keep an eye on things for you.'

'What nonsense!' said Mrs. Pepperpot. She tried to stand up, but it was rather difficult with her dress caught in the trap and she herself so tiny.

'Take it easy, Queen of the House,' said the big mouse. 'Let my son here tell you what he has seen.'

Timidly, one of the little mice came forward and told how he had climbed up the chimney one day and peeped through a hole into the kitchen. There he had seen a terrible monster who was eating up all the cake in the tin.

Then the other little mouse chirped in to tell how he had been playing hide-and-seek behind a jam-jar on the shelf when the monster had put out a huge hand and taken the jar away. But he had been so scared when he saw the little mouse that he had dropped the jar on the floor, and all the bramble jelly came pouring out.

Suddenly they heard Tramp! Tramp! Tramp! up above; the sound of huge boots walking about.

'That's the monster!' said one of the little mice.

'Yes, that's him all right!' said the other little mouse.

'Is it, indeed!' said Mrs. Pepperpot. 'If only I could get out of this trap, I should very much like to go and have a look at this monster.'

'We'll help you,' said all the mice, and they set to work to free Mrs. Pepperpot from the trap in the way only mice know how; they gnawed through her skirt, leaving a piece stuck in the spring.

'Now you must hurry up to the kitchen to see the monster,' they said.

'But how am I to get there?' asked Mrs. Pepperpot.

'Up through the chimney on our special rope; we'll pull you up.'

And that's what they did. They hoisted Mrs. Pepperpot higher and higher inside the chimney, until she could see a chink of light.

'That's the crack into the kitchen,' the big mouse told her from below.

She called down to him: 'Thank you Mr. Watchman, thank you for your help, and keep a sharp look-out!'

Then she climbed through the hole in the wall. As soon as she set foot on the floor she grew to her normal size. Standing in front of the stove, she put her hands on her hips and said, 'So it's you, husband, is it, who's been eating all my short-cake and stealing the bramble jelly in the cellar?'

Mr. Pepperpot looked dumbfounded: 'How did you know that?' he said.

'Because I have a watchman now, I have paid him a penny,' said Mrs. Pepperpot.

The bad luck story

IF YOU take the road past Mrs. Pepperpot's house and turn to the right, then to the left and carry straight on, you will come to a cottage.

In this cottage lived an old woman they called 'Mrs. Calamity', because she believed in omens and always expected the worst to happen. Another curious thing about her was that she had the habit of stealing cuttings from pot-plants in other people's houses. Not that this in itself was very serious, only sometimes the flowers died after she had been cutting them about. But Mrs. Calamity had the idea that stolen plants thrive much better than any you got as a present, which is just one of those old wives' tales.

One day she visited little old Mrs. Pepperpot. She sat on the edge of a chair very politely and talked about this and that, but all the time she was looking round at all the plants in Mrs. Pepperpot's window-sill.

'That's right; have a good look,' thought Mrs. Pepperpot to herself. 'I know what you're after; you want to take cuttings of my best geranium. But we'll see about that, my fine lady!'

Unfortunately, there was a knock at the door just at that moment, and Mrs. Pepperpot had to leave her visitor alone while she went to answer it.

A man stood there. 'Anyone called Cuthbertson live here?' he asked.

'Cuthbertson? There's never been anyone of that name in this house, as far as I know,' said Mrs. Pepperpot. 'You'd better ask at the post-office. Excuse me, I'm busy just now.' And she turned to shut the door.

Too late! For at that moment Mrs. Pepperpot shrank again!

She stretched her little neck as much as she could to look over the doorstep into the sitting-room. Sure enough! There was Mrs. Calamity ferreting about in Mrs. Pepperpot's flowerpots.

'I have a feeling you're going to regret that, Madam Thief,' thought Mrs. Pepperpot as she swung herself over the step into the yard. There she found a little wagtail pecking about, looking for something to eat.

'Hullo, little wagtail,' she said. 'If you'll help *me*, then I'll help *you*. You can have all the crumbs you want if you'll just go over to the front doorstep and stand quite still, facing the door.'

'That's easily done,' said the wagtail, and hopped across the yard.

No doubt Mrs. Calamity was wondering what had happened to the lady of the house. She came to the door and looked out, holding her hand carefully over her apron pocket where she had hidden the geranium cutting.

Then she caught sight of the wagtail on the step. 'Oh Calamity!' she wailed. 'I've looked a wagtail straight in the face and now I shall have bad luck for a year.'

And, clutching her apron pocket, she hurried away from the house.

But over her head the wagtail was following her, flying with Mrs. Pepperpot on its back. As she clung with her arms round the bird's neck, she said: 'D'you know where we could find a black cat?'

'A black cat?' answered the wagtail. 'I should think I do! The horrible creature was lying in wait for me down by the bend in the road. She's probably still there. So don't ask me to land anywhere near her.'

'Don't worry!' said Mrs. Pepperpot. 'I want you to put me down on the *opposite* side of the road—I have a little plan.'

So the wagtail did as she asked and flew out of harm's way as fast as it could go.

Mrs. Pepperpot crouched down in the long grass; she could see the cat's tail waving to and fro in the ditch

on the other side of the road. Soon she heard the clump, clump, clump of Mrs. Calamity's boots as she walked down the road.

Just as she came past where Mrs. Pepperpot was

hiding, Mrs. Pepperpot made the noise of a wagtail calling. The black cat heard it and, like a streak of lightning, shot across the road, right in front of Mrs. Calamity.

Mrs. Calamity stood stock-still with fright. 'A black cat!' she screamed. 'That means *three* years' bad luck!

Oh Calamity, what shall I do?' She was so alarmed she didn't dare go on; instead, she took the path through the wood to her house.

Meanwhile the cat was going in the same direction, for by now Mrs. Pepperpot was riding on her back. 'Have you seen any magpies about?' she asked the cat.

'I should think I have!' said the cat. 'There's a pair of them in that birch-tree over there; they tease me and pull my tail whenever they get the chance. Look! They're waiting for me now!'

'Then you can drop me here,' said Mrs. Pepperpot. 'Come and see me tomorrow and I'll give you a bowl of cream.'

The cat did as she asked, and a moment later Mrs. Pepperpot was talking to the magpies in the birch-tree.

'Good afternoon,' she said. 'I wonder if you would have such a thing as a key-ring in your nest?'

'Oh no,' said the magpies, 'we don't have key-rings, we only collect broken-mirror bits.'

'The best is good enough,' replied Mrs. Pepperpot. 'I want you to put some nice-looking bits on Mrs. Calamity's doorstep. If you can do that for me, I'll keep the curly tail for you when we kill the pig at Christmas.'

The magpies didn't need to be told twice. A little heap of broken-mirror bits were on Mrs. Calamity's doorstep before you could say Jack Robinson.

When she arrived and saw what was waiting for her Mrs. Calamity sat down and cried.

'Oh, misery me! Oh Calamity! A broken mirror will give me *seven* years' bad luck!'

But by now Mrs. Pepperpot had grown to her proper size again; quietly she came round the corner, and her voice was quite gentle when she spoke.

'Now, now, Mrs. Calamity,' she said, 'you mustn't sit here crying.'

'Oh, Mrs. Pepperpot! It's nothing but bad luck for me from beginning to end.' She sniffed, and she told Mrs. Pepperpot about the wagtail that had faced her, the cat that had jumped across her path and now the broken mirror. When she'd finished she fished for a handkerchief in her apron pocket.

Out fell the geranium cutting!

Mrs. Calamity picked it up and handed it to Mrs. Pepperpot. 'There—take it! I stole it from your house. Now you'd better have it back, for I shall never need geraniums or anything else in this world, I don't suppose!'

'Don't be silly,' said Mrs. Pepperpot. 'Let's forget about all this nonsense, shall we? I'm going to *give* you the cutting as a present. You plant it, and I'm sure you'll find that it'll grow into the finest flower you ever had.'

She was right. The tiny cutting grew into a huge geranium with bright red blooms, and that in spite of the fact that Mrs. Calamity not only thanked Mrs. Pepperpot, but shook hands as well, which is the worst thing you can do if you believe in bad omens.

But from then on she changed her ideas, and people no longer called her Mrs. Calamity, but plain Mrs. Brown instead.

Mrs. Pepperpot and the moose

It was winter-time, and Mrs. Pepperpot was having trouble getting water. The tap in her kitchen ran slower and slower, until one day it just dripped and then stopped altogether. The well was empty.

'Ah, well,' thought Mrs. Pepperpot, 'it won't be the first time I've had this kind of trouble, and it won't be the last. But with two strong arms and a good sound bucket, not to mention the lucky chance that there's another well down by the forest fence, we'll soon fix that.'

So she put on her husband's old winter coat and a pair of thick gloves and fetched a pick-axe from the wood-shed. Then she trudged through the snow down the hill, to where there was a dip by the forest fence. She swept the snow away and started breaking a hole in the ice with the pick-axe. Chips of ice flew everywhere as Mrs. Pepperpot hacked away, not looking to left or right. She made such a noise that she never heard the sound of breaking twigs, nor the snorting that was coming from the other side of the fence.

But there he was; a huge moose with great big antlers, not moving at all, but staring angrily at Mrs. Pepperpot. Suddenly he gave a very loud snort and leaped over the fence, butting Mrs. Pepperpot from behind, so that she went head-first into a pile of snow!

'What the dickens!' cried Mrs. Pepperpot as she scrambled to her feet. But by that time the moose was back on the other side of the fence. When she saw what

it was that had pushed her over, Mrs. Pepperpot lost no time in scrambling up the hill and into her house, locking the door behind her. Then she peeped out of the kitchen window to see if the moose was still there. He was.

'You wait, you great big brute!' said Mrs. Pepperpot. 'I'll give you a fright you won't forget!'

She put on a black rain-cape and a battered old hat, and in her hand she carried a big stick. Then she crept out of the door and hid round the corner of the house.

The moose was quietly nibbling the bark off the trees and seemed to be taking no notice of her.

Suddenly she stormed down the hill, shouting, 'Woollah, Woollah, Woollah!' like a Red Indian, the black rain-cape flapping round her and the stick waving in the air. The moose *should* have been frightened, but he just took one look at the whirling thing coming towards him, leaped the fence and headed straight for it!

Poor Mrs. Pepperpot! All she could do was to rush back indoors again as fast as she knew how.

'Now what shall I do?' she wondered. 'I must have water to cook my potatoes and do my washing-up, and a little cup of coffee wouldn't come amiss after all this excitement. Perhaps if I were to put on my old man's trousers and take his gun out . . . I could pretend to aim it; that might scare him off.'

So she put on the trousers and took out the gun; but this was the silliest idea she had had yet, because, before she was half-way down the hill, that moose came pounding towards her on his great long legs. She never had time to point the gun. Worse still, she dropped it in her efforts to keep the trousers up and run back to the house at the same time. When the moose saw her disappear indoors, he turned and stalked down the hill again, but this time he didn't jump back over the fence, but stayed by the well, as if he were guarding it.

'Ah well,' said Mrs. Pepperpot, 'I suppose I shall have to fill the bucket with snow and melt it to get the water I need. That moose is clearly not afraid of anything.'

So she took her bucket and went outside. But just as she was bending down to scoop up the snow, she turned small! But this time the magic worked quicker than usual, and somehow she managed to tumble into the bucket which was lying on its side. The bucket started to roll down the hill; faster and faster it went, and poor Mrs. Pepperpot was seeing stars as she bumped round and round inside.

Just above the dip near the well a little mound jutted out, and here the bucket made a leap into space. 'This is the end of me!' thought Mrs. Pepperpot. She waited for the bump, but it didn't come! Instead the bucket seemed to be floating through the air, over the

fence and right into the forest. If she had had time to think, Mrs. Pepperpot would have known that the moose had somehow caught the bucket on one of his antlers, but it is not so easy to think when you're swinging between heaven and earth.

At last the bucket got stuck on a branch and the moose thundered on through the undergrowth. Mrs. Pepperpot lay there panting, trying to get her breath back. She had no idea where she was. But then she heard: 'Chuck, chuck! Chuck, chuck!'—the chattering of a squirrel as he ran down the tree-trunk over her head.

'Hullo!' said the squirrel, 'if it isn't Mrs. Pepperpot! Out for a walk, or something?'

'Not exactly a *walk*,' said Mrs. Pepperpot, 'but I've had a free ride, though I don't know who gave it to me.'

'That was the King of the Moose,' said the squirrel. 'I saw him gallop past with a wild look in his eyes. It's the first time I have ever seen him afraid, I can tell you that. He is so stupid and so stuck-up you wouldn't believe it. All he thinks of is fighting; he goes for anything and anybody—the bigger the better. But you seem to have given him the fright of his life.'

'I'm glad I managed it in the end,' said Mrs. Pepperpot, 'and now I'd be gladder still if I knew how to get myself home.'

But she needn't have worried, because at that moment she felt herself grow large again, and the next thing she knew she had broken the branch and was lying on the ground. She picked herself and her bucket up and started walking home. But when she got to the fence she took a turn down to the well to fill the bucket.

When she stood up she looked back towards the forest, and there, sure enough, stood the moose, blinking at her. But Mrs. Pepperpot was no longer afraid of him. All she had to do was to rattle that bucket a little, and the big creature shook his head and disappeared silently into the forest.

From that day on Mrs. Pepperpot had no trouble fetching water from the well by the forest fence.

Mrs. Pepperpot finds a hidden treasure

It was a fine sunny day in January, and Mrs. Pepperpot was peeling potatoes at the kitchen sink.

'Miaow!' said the cat; she was lying in front of the stove.

'Miaow yourself!' answered Mrs. Pepperpot.

'Miaow!' said the cat again.

Mrs. Pepperpot suddenly remembered an old, old rhyme she learned when she was a child. It went like this:

The cat sat by the fire,
Her aches and pains were dire,
Such throbbing in my head,
She cried; I'll soon be dead!

'Poor Pussy! Are your aches and pains so bad? Does your head throb?' she said, and smiled down at the cat.

But the cat only looked at her.

Mrs. Pepperpot stopped peeling potatoes, wiped her hands and knelt down beside the cat. 'There's something you want to tell me, isn't there, Pussy? It's too bad I can't understand you except when I'm little, but it's not my fault.' She stroked the cat, but Pussy didn't purr, just went on looking at her.

'Well, I can't spend all day being sorry for you, my girl, I've got a husband to feed,' said Mrs. Pepperpot, and went back to the potatoes in the sink. When they were ready she put them in a saucepan of cold water on the stove, not forgetting a good pinch of salt. After that she laid the table, for her husband had to have his dinner sharp at one o'clock and it was now half past twelve.

Pussy was at the door now. 'Miaow!' she said, scratching at it.

'You want to get out, do you?' said Mrs. Pepperpot, and opened the door. She followed the cat out, because she had noticed that her broom had fallen over in the snow. The door closed behind her.

And at that moment she shrank to her pepperpot size!

'About time too!' said the cat. 'I've been waiting for days for this to happen. Now don't let's waste any more time; jump on my back! We're setting off at once.'

Mrs. Pepperpot didn't stop to ask where they were going; she climbed on Pussy's back. 'Hold on tight!' said Pussy, and bounded off down the little bank at the back of the house past Mrs. Pepperpot's rubbish-heap.

'We're coming to the first hindrance,' said Pussy; 'just sit tight and don't say a word!' All Mrs. Pepperpot could see was a single birch-tree with a couple of magpies on it. True, the birds seemed as big as eagles to her now and the tree was like a mountain. But when the magpies started screeching she knew what the cat meant.

'There's the cat! There's the cat!' they screamed. 'Let's nip her tail! Let's pull her whiskers!' And they swooped down, skimming so close over Mrs. Pepperpot's head she was nearly blown off the cat's back. But the cat took no notice at all, just kept steadily on down the hill, and the magpies soon tired of the game.

'That's that!' said the cat. 'The next thing we have to watch out for is being hit by snowballs. We have to cross the boys' playground now, so if any of them start aiming at you, duck behind my ears and hang on!'

Mrs. Pepperpot looked at the boys; she knew them all, she had often given them sweets and biscuits. '*They* can't be dangerous,' she said to herself.

But then she heard one of them say: 'There comes that stupid cat; let's see who can hit it first! Come on,

boys!' And they all started pelting snowballs as hard as they could.

Suddenly remembering how small she was, Mrs. Pepperpot did as the cat had told her and crouched down behind Pussy's ears until they were safely out of range.

The cat ran on till they got to a wire fence with a hole just big enough for her to wriggle through.

'So far, so good,' she said, 'but now comes the worst bit, because this is dog land, and we don't want to get caught. So keep your eyes skinned!'

The fence divided Mrs. Pepperpot's land from her neighbour's, but she knew the neighbour's dog quite well; he had had many a bone and scraps from her and he was always very friendly. 'We'll be all right here,' she thought.

But she was wrong. Without any warning, that dog suddenly came bearing down on them in great leaps and bounds! Mrs. Pepperpot shook like a jelly when she saw his wide-open jaws all red, with sharp, white teeth glistening in a terrifying way. She flattened herself on the cat's back and clung on for dear life, for Pussy shot like a Sputnik across the yard and straight under the neighbour's barn.

'Phew!' said the cat, 'that was a narrow squeak! Thanks very much for coming all this way with me; I'm afraid it wasn't a very comfortable journey.'

'That's all right,' said Mrs. Pepperpot, 'but perhaps you'll tell me now what we've come for?'

'It's a surprise,' said Pussy, 'but don't worry, you'll get your reward. All we have to do now is to find the hidden treasure, but that means crawling through the hay. So hang on!'

And off they went again, slowly this time, for it was difficult to make their way through the prickly stalks that seemed as big as bean-poles to Mrs. Pepperpot. The dust was terrible; it went in her eyes, her mouth, her hair, down her neck—everywhere.

'Can you see anything?' asked the cat.

'Only blackness,' answered Mrs. Pepperpot, 'and it seems to be getting blacker.'

'In that case we're probably going the right way,' said Pussy, crawling further into the hay. 'D'you see anything now?' she asked.

'Nothing at all,' said Mrs. Pepperpot, for by now her eyes were completely bunged up with hay-seed and dust.

'Try rubbing your eyes,' said the cat, 'for this is where your hidden treasure is.'

So Mrs. Pepperpot rubbed her eyes, blinked and rubbed again until at last she could open them properly. When she did, she was astonished; all round her shone the most wonderful jewels! Diamonds, sapphires, emeralds—they glittered in every hue!

'There you are! Didn't I tell you I had a hidden treasure for you?' said the cat, but she didn't give Mrs. Pepperpot time to have a closer look. 'We'll have to hurry back now, it's nearly time for your husband's dinner.'

So they crawled back through the hay and, just as they got out in the daylight, Mrs. Pepperpot grew to her ordinary size. She picked the cat up in her arms and walked across the yard with her. The dog was there, but what a different dog! He nuzzled Mrs. Pepperpot's skirt and wagged his tail in the friendliest way.

Through the gate they came to the place where the boys were playing. Everyone of them nodded to her and politely said 'Good morning'. Then they went on up the hill, and there were the magpies in the birch-tree. But not a sound came from them; they didn't even seem to notice them walking by.

When they got to the house Mrs. Pepperpot put the cat down and hurried indoors. It was almost one o'clock. She snatched the saucepan from the stove—a few potatoes had stuck to the bottom, so she threw those

out and emptied the rest into a blue serving-bowl. The saucepan she put outside the back door with cold water in it.

She had only just got everything ready when Mr. Pepperpot came in. He sniffed suspiciously. 'I can smell burnt potatoes,' he said.

'Nonsense,' said Mrs. Pepperpot, 'I dropped a bit of potato-skin on the stove, that's all. But I've aired the room since, so just you sit down and eat your dinner.'

'Aren't you having any?' asked her husband.

'Not just now,' answered Mrs. Pepperpot, 'I have to go and fetch something first. I won't be long.' And Mrs. Pepperpot went back down the hill, through the gate to her neighbour's yard, and into the barn. But this time she climbed *over* the hay till she found the spot where her hidden treasure lay.

And what d'you think it was?

Four coal-black kittens with shining eyes!

Mr. Pepperpot

Now you have heard a lot about *Mrs.* Pepperpot, but hardly anything about *Mr.* Pepperpot.

He usually comes in at the end of the stories, when Mrs. Pepperpot is back to her normal size and busy with his dinner. If the food isn't ready he always says 'Can't a man ever get his dinner at the proper time in this house?' And if it is ready, he just sits down to eat and says nothing at all. If it's cold out, he says 'Brrrrrrr!' and if it's very hot, he says 'Pheeew!' If Mrs. Pepperpot has done something he doesn't like, he says 'Hmmmmm!' in a disapproving tone of voice. But if he himself is thinking of doing something he doesn't want Mrs. Pepperpot to know about, he goes round the house whistling to himself and humming a little tune.

One evening when he came home, he went up to the attic. Now, Mrs. Pepperpot had hidden four black kittens up there, because Mr. Pepperpot didn't like kittens when they were small (some people don't, you know). So, when Mr. Pepperpot came down from the attic, he stood in the middle of the floor and said 'Hmmmm!' And a little while later he started whistling and humming his tune.

Mrs. Pepperpot said nothing, though she knew what it meant. She just took his old winter coat from its peg and started mending a tear in it.

'What are you mending that for?' asked Mr. Pepperpot.

'The weather's getting so bad, you'll need it,' said Mrs. Pepperpot.

'Who said I was going out?' asked Mr. Pepperpot.

'You can do as you like,' said his wife, 'I'm staying right where I am.'

'Well, maybe I *will* take a turn outside, all the same,' said Mr. Pepperpot.

'I thought you would,' she said.

Mr. Pepperpot went back to the attic, found a big sack and popped the four kittens inside. But when he got to the bottom of the stairs, he thought he would put on the old winter coat. So he put the sack down and went into the kitchen. There he found the coat hanging over a chair.

'I'm going out now!' he called, thinking his wife must be in the sitting-room. He got no answer, but he didn't bother to call again, as he was afraid the kittens might get out of the sack which wasn't properly tied. Quickly he slung it over his shoulder and went out.

It was a nasty night; the wind blew sleet in his face and the road was full of icy puddles.

'Ugh!' said Mr. Pepperpot, 'this weather's fit to drown in!'

'Isn't that just what you're going to do to us poor kittens?' said a tiny voice close by.

Mr. Pepperpot was startled. 'Who said that, I wonder?' he said. He put the sack down to look inside, but as soon as he opened it out jumped one of the kittens and ran off in the darkness.

'Oh dear, what shall I do?' he said, tying up the sack again as quickly as he could. 'I can't leave a kitten running about on a night like this.'

'He won't get any wetter than the rest of us by the time you've finished with us,' said the little voice again.

Mr. Pepperpot untied the sack once more to find out who was speaking. Out jumped the second kitten and disappeared in the sleet and snow. While he hurriedly tied a knot to stop the rest from getting out, he said to himself:

'What if the fox got those two little mites? That would be terrible!'

'No worse than being in *your* hands,' said the tiny voice.

This time, Mr. Pepperpot was very careful to hold his hand over the opening as he untied it. But his foot slipped on the ice and jogged the sack out of his hand, and another kitten got away.

'Three gone! That's bad!' he said.

'Not as bad as it'll be for me!' came the voice from the sack.

'I know who it is now,' said Mr. Pepperpot; 'it's my

old woman who's shrunk again. You're in that sack, aren't you? But I'll catch you! You just wait!' And with that he opened the sack again.

Out jumped the fourth kitten and ran off, lickety-split!

'You can run, I don't care!' said the old man. 'I'm going to catch that wife of mine—it's all her fault!' He got down on his knees and rummaged round in every corner of the sack. But he found nothing—it was quite empty.

Now he really was worried; he was so worried he started sobbing and crying, and in between he called 'Puss, Puss!' and searched all over the place.

A little girl came along the road. 'What have you lost?' she asked.

'Some kittens,' sniffed Mr. Pepperpot.

'I'll help you find them,' said the little girl.

Soon they were joined by a little boy, and he had a torch which made it easier to search. First the little girl found one kitten behind a tree-stump, then the boy found two kittens stuck in a snow-drift, and Mr. Pepperpot himself found the fourth one and put them all back in the sack, tying it very securely this time.

'Thank you for your help,' he said to the children and asked them to take the kittens back to his house and put them in the kitchen.

When they had gone, he started looking for his little old woman. He searched for an hour—for two hours; he called, he begged, he sobbed, he was quite beside himself. But in the end he had to give up. 'I'll go home now,' he said to himself, 'and try again tomorrow.'

But when he got home, there was Mrs. Pepperpot, as large as life, bustling round the kitchen, frying a huge pile of pancakes! And by the kitchen stove was a wicker basket with the mother cat and all four kittens in it.

'When did you come home?' asked the astonished Mr. Pepperpot.

'When did I come home? Why, I've been here all the time, of course,' she said.

'But who was it talking to me from the sack, then?'

'I've no idea,' said Mrs. Pepperpot, 'unless it was your conscience.' And she came over and gave him a great big hug and kiss.

Then Mr. Pepperpot sat down to eat the biggest pile of pancakes he had ever had and all with bilberry jam, and when he was full the kittens finished off the last four.

And after that Mr. and Mrs. Pepperpot lived happily together, and Mrs. Pepperpot gave up shrinking for a very long time indeed—that's why the next story is a made-up story about an OGRE and not about Mrs. Pepperpot at all, at all.

The ogres

IT IS time we made up a story about *ogres.* You see we have to make it up, because there aren't any ogres, really.

First we must have an ogre and he must have a name. Let's call him GAPY GOB, because he's very fond of eating and is always opening his mouth for more.

Good. Gapy Gob has two servants, a little girl and a little boy. The little girl spends all *her* time cooking porridge for her master, so we can call her KATIE COOK. The little boy spends all *his* time chopping wood to burn in the stove on which Katie cooks the porridge. So we can call him CHARLIE CHOP.

Katie Cook and Charlie Chop aren't really ogres at all; they're just ordinary children, but they have no home of their own, so Gapy Gob lets them stay with him. They are very happy there, except for one thing; on the other side of the hill lives an ogress by the name of WILY WINNIE and her servant, a very cunning cat called RIBBY RATSOUP.

Now I think we have enough ogres and people to start the story, don't you?

Wily Winnie was very set on marrying Gapy Gob, because she knew he had a large ham hanging in his larder. Not only that, but Gapy Gob had a much better house than her own and she wanted to live in it. But first she had to get rid of the ogre's two servants, Katie Cook and Charlie Chop.

Several times she had tried to persuade him to send them away, but each time the children had told Gapy Gob that Wily Winnie was just after his ham and that her cat was waiting to eat up all the herrings they had salted down.

One morning early, when Gapy Gob was sitting at the table waiting for Katie to finish stirring his porridge, and

Charlie was sharpening his axe ready for the day's work, there was a knock at the door.

'Come in,' said Katie.

The door opened, and there stood Ribby Ratsoup, Wily Winnie's cat.

'Good morning,' she said, trying to curtsey politely, but it was difficult because she was wearing riding-boots and carried a large bucket over one paw.

'Good morning,' said Katie. 'If you've brought that

bucket for salt herrings, you can spare yourself the trouble; you're not having any.'

'No, no, nothing of the kind!' said the cat. 'I just called to see if anyone here would like to go bilberry-picking with me.'

'Bilberry-picking?' said Gapy Gob. 'You going bilberry-picking? What a clever cat you are! But I don't think Katie and Charlie have time to go with you today.' The ogre was a bit put out because he had had to wait for his porridge.

'I was just asking,' said Ribby in a sugary voice. 'You see, at *our* house we get up early. I get all the work done before breakfast. So my mistress told me to go berrying today, and of course I do as I am told. Well, bye-bye for now!'

When the cat had gone, the ogre said, 'I don't really see why you shouldn't go bilberrying too; they're very nice to eat. . . .' And he licked his chops.

'Just as you like,' said Charlie. 'We don't mind going. But then you'll have to look after yourself while we're out.'

'Don't touch the matches, whatever you do!' warned Katie.

'And if anybody knocks, be sure *not* to open the door,' said Charlie.

'I won't,' said Gapy Gob.

But as soon as the children had gone, Wily Winnie came panting over the hill, her skirts flying.

'Hullo, hullo! How are you, Gapy Gob?' she shouted, and marched straight into the kitchen.

Gapy Gob backed away from her into a corner. 'I'm not supposed to open the door if anyone knocks,' he said.

'Ah, but I *didn't* knock. I came straight in!' said the ogress. 'How nice to see you again, dear Gapy Gob. My cat has gone bilberry-picking, so I was all alone!'

'The children have gone as well,' said Gapy Gob.

'How lovely!' cried Wily Winnie. 'Then you can come home with me for a while. We can sit and talk while we wait for them to bring back the berries. I wonder who will bring the most? Come along now, Gapy, let me help you on with your coat. First this arm; that's right, and now this one. There now, we're ready to go!'

So Gapy Gob went home with Wily Winnie and sat in her house all day, while Katie Cook and Charlie Chop searched the wood for all the bilberries they could find. They each had a punnet to pick in, and when they were full they tipped them into their bucket which stood under a fir-tree.

But what d'you think Ribby Ratsoup had been doing all this time? Well, she hadn't been picking bilberries, I

can tell you that much! She spent the day scampering through the forest, chasing squirrels and field mice and birds. Late in the afternoon she came across the children's bucket, filled almost to the brim with bilberries. Katie and Charlie were out of sight, picking their last punnet each.

Ribby, as I told you before, was a very cunning cat. She emptied all the berries into her own bucket and one of her boots. Then she ran home to her mistress as fast as she could go.

Back in Wily Winnie's house the ogre and ogress were getting on fine together. They had come to an agreement that if the *cat* came home with most bilberries, Gapy

Gob would send Katie and Charlie away, but if the *children* had most, Ribby Ratsoup would have to go.

Suddenly they saw something come streaking across the hill-top. It was the cat with her bucket and her boot full of bilberries.

Wily Winnie clapped her hands. 'My cat's won! My cat's won! Look what a lot she's brought!'

'Ah, you wait and see what the children bring!' said Gapy Gob. He was so fond of the children, he didn't want to lose them.

A little while later they saw Katie and Charlie come over the hill-top. But they were walking very, very slowly. And their bucket was—empty.

'What did I tell you, Gapy Gob?' shouted the ogress. 'Those children are no good. Send them away, Gapy, send them away!'

So Gapy Gob went out in the yard and said to the

children: 'Charlie and Katie, you can go. I don't want you any more; you can't even pick bilberries.' And he turned away, for he had tears in his eyes.

'I see,' said Charlie.

'Very well,' said Katie.

'Ribby is much better at picking than you are,' said Gapy Gob.

'Is that so?' said Charlie. 'Then perhaps Madam Ratsoup wouldn't mind showing us her paws?'

'My paws?' said the cat. 'Certainly you can see my paws.' And she held them up.

'Hmm!' said Charlie. 'Very strange. The cat has picked a whole bucket and a boot full, yet her paws are as clean as if she'd been licking them all day. *We*, who have no bilberries to show for it, have our arms stained blue right up to the elbows. Ribby Ratsoup is a thief; she has stolen our berries and now she can give them back to us, every single one, or it will be the worse for her!'

The cat saw the game was up and quickly handed back the berries. Then the children took Gapy Gob by the hands and they all three went home together.

But Wily Winnie was so angry, she shut the cat up in the barn without any supper.

That's the end of this story. Now it's your turn to make one up about the ogres, and we'll see which is the best.

The good luck story

ONCE upon a time there was a little old woman—no, what am I saying? She was a little girl. But this little girl worked every bit as hard as any grown-up woman. Her name was Betsy; she wore a scarf round her head like the women did, and she could weed a field of turnips with the best of them. If any of the big boys started throwing stones or lumps of earth at her, she tossed her head and gave them a piece of her mind.

She was weeding in the field one day when a lady-bird settled on her hand.

'Poor little ladybird! What do you want on my thumb?' said Betsy, at the same time trying to think of a really good wish. For ever since she was tiny she had been told to make a wish when a ladybird flew from her finger.

'I wish . . . I wish I had a new skipping-rope to take to school,' she said quickly. But then she remembered that she had borrowed a skipping-rope from her friend, Anna, and lost it. If she got a new one now she would *have* to give it to Anna.

The ladybird crawled slowly out on Betsy's thumb-nail, and she was terrified it would fly away before she had had time to wish for all the things she wanted. Luckily, the ladybird changed its mind when it reached the top; it crawled down again and started up the first finger.

'Now I shall wish—I wish I could have some money,' said Betsy, but was sorry as soon as she had said it. After all, she would *get* some money when she had finished her weeding. And, anyway, the money would have to go to Britta from Hill Farm to pay for the old bicycle Betsy had bought from her in the spring.

The ladybird crawled right out on the top of Betsy's first finger. Then it stopped to consider, and slowly

turned round and climbed down again to start on the second finger.

'Now I must hurry up and wish before it flies off the top of this finger,' said Betsy, while the ladybird climbed steadily upwards.

'I wish I were a real princess,' she said, but then she thought: 'How stupid of me—how can I be a real princess if I haven't been one before? Unless, of course, a prince came along and asked me to marry him. That would look funny, wouldn't it? A prince in a turnip field!' And she laughed at herself.

The ladybird was stretching one wing now and hovering.

'Don't fly yet, little ladybird! I don't want to be a princess at all. I want something quite different. I want my mother to be rid of her rheumatics when I get home tonight.'

This was a good wish, and Betsy was pleased with it. You see, it was a great trouble to her when her mother had the rheumatics; then Betsy had to dress all her little brothers and sisters and give them their dinner. It would be nice not to have to work so hard.

But the ladybird didn't take off even from this finger. Slowly it turned round and made its way to the bottom of the finger and then on to Betsy's hand. Then it stopped; it didn't seem to want to go on at all. But Betsy gave it a gentle little push and got it on to her third finger.

Now she knew what to wish; that her father could get the job he was after that day. Because if he did, he had said he would buy her a whole sheet of pictures to stick in her scrap-book.

But the ladybird had its own ideas; it crawled more and more slowly up Betsy's third finger, and every now and then Betsy had to poke it to get it out on the nail. Then all of a sudden the ladybird rolled off and fell on to the ground.

Betsy lay down flat among the turnips and managed to coax the creature on to her little finger. It didn't move. So Betsy lifted it gingerly out on the nail. Still it didn't move, and she thought she must have hurt it. 'You poor thing! Did I squeeze you too hard? Oh, please, little ladybird, do fly now! Because I want to wish that Daddy could get the job he's after!'

And suddenly the ladybird opened its wings and flew off—straight up towards the sun.

And do you know? When Betsy got home that night her mother was feeling better than she had been for a long while. Her father had got the job and had remembered the pictures for her scrap-book, and her friend Anna had been to see her. She had found the lost skipping-rope and brought it for Betsy, because she had a new one herself. Not only that, but Britta from Hill Farm had been to say that if Betsy would mind her baby for her twice that week, she needn't pay any more for the old bicycle!

What more could you want from a lucky ladybird?

Mr. Big Toe's journey

MR. BIG TOE lived with his four brothers in a little sock, and the sock lived in a shoe which belonged to a little boy who was walking down the lane eating a very big sandwich.

Mr. Big Toe said: 'Now I've been stuck in this place so long, I think it's time I did some travelling.'

When his brothers asked him where he was going, he answered: 'Oh, I expect I shall sail across the ocean.'

'But how will you get through the wall?' they asked him—they meant the sock, of course.

'That's easy for someone as big as I am. I shall just scratch a hole.'

'Will we never see you again?' asked the one who was closest to Mr. Big Toe.

'Maybe not. But I'll ring you up and tell you how I'm getting on. Well, I'm off now, so goodbye!'

Then Mr. Big Toe started scratching a hole, and it didn't take long before he had wriggled through. The rest of the toes sat waiting for the telephone message.

Soon the little boy started running and Mr. Big Toe sent his first message:

'Hullo, hullo! I've started on my travels. It feels rather strange at first, of course, and I miss you a bit. But I expect you miss me much more. Be good. I'll ring you up again when I get on the boat.'

After a time the little boy found a puddle and began dipping his shoe in it. Mr. Big Toe got on the telephone again.

'Hullo boys, I've just got to the edge of the ocean; in a few moments I'll be sailing to the far shore. It's a dangerous journey, but don't worry, I'll manage! The waves are enormous! Still, the boat seems strong and seaworthy. It won't be long now before I meet the African Chief's Big Toe and all his little black brothers. I'll tell them I've left *my* four brothers at home. They'll be glad to hear about you, I expect. . . . Bye, bye, I must ring off now till we get to the far shore.'

The boy waded out into the middle of the puddle, but it was deeper than he thought, and while the other toes were lying inside the sock, thinking of their big brother alone on the stormy sea, they had another call from him.

'Hullo there! This is getting more and more dangerous; the boat is out in the middle of the ocean, and it's leaking badly. If you don't hear anything more for a

bit, it's because I have to use my nail to bail the water out. It's difficult, but I'm not a bit afraid!'

'Poor Big Toe!' the brothers said to each other and huddled closer together inside the sock.

The little boy had splashed through the puddle by now. Next he found a tricycle and got on it. He rode it as fast as he could and stuck both his legs straight out in the air.

Mr. Big Toe's telephone rang again. 'Hullo boys, hullo! It's your brother Big Toe calling. I'm floating in mid-air. I'm in an aeroplane, but you needn't worry, it's quite safe. The boat sank, though I did my best to bail all the water out. I was alone, you see, that made it very difficult. However, you'll be pleased to know I'm on my way home now. See you all soon!'

The boy went indoors to change his wet socks. The five toes got a new home to live in and the boy set out again with another big sandwich in his hand.

'Fancy you coming home to us!' said all the brothers to Mr. Big Toe, and they curled themselves round him to make him feel warm and cosy.

'Yes, yes, home is all right when the sock is dry and clean,' said Mr. Big Toe. 'But I don't suppose it will be long before I take another journey.'

A concertina concert

Do you remember the story we made up? The one about the ogres, Gapy Gob and Wily Winnie? Gapy Gob had two servants, Katie Cook and Charlie Chop, who were not ogres at all, but just ordinary children. Wily Winnie had a cat to look after her, called Ribby Ratsoup, a very cunning cat. These two would sit at home in the evenings and talk about how they could get Gapy Gob to marry Wily Winnie. Then one day, just after New Year, the cat had an idea.

'I know how to get Gapy Gob to marry you,' she said. 'Tell him you have learned to play the concertina. Gapy likes concertina music better than anything.'

'You have some bright ideas, I must say!' said Wily Winnie scornfully. 'You know I can't play the concertina.'

'Don't worry about that,' said Ribby. 'I met a musician in the forest this morning; that's what made me think of it. Wait here till I fetch him.'

So the cat went into the forest and there, under a fir-tree, sat a very small, thin musician. He had been

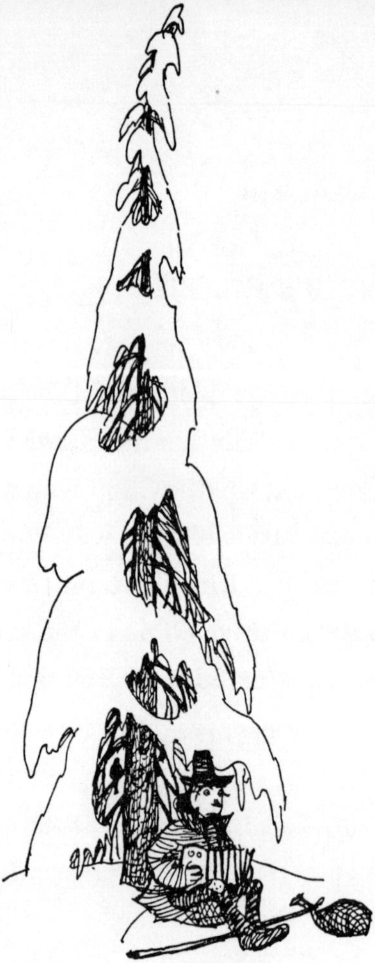

playing his concertina at village gatherings all through Christmas and now he was anxious to get home as quickly as possible. But when Ribby had met him that morning, the little musician had lost his way in the forest. So Ribby had promised to come back and guide him if he would wait there.

'You can play me a tune in return,' the cat had said.

Now, when the musician saw the cat trotting towards him he was very pleased.

'Shall I play you a tune now?' he asked.

'Not just yet,' said Ribby. 'I want you to come home with me first to eat a meal and have some coffee. Then you can play your concertina to me and my mistress.'

This sounded a good idea to the musician, who was hungry by now. But when he got to the door and saw that the cat's mistress was an ogress, he was very frightened.

At first Wily Winnie did her best to be nice to him, but as this only made him more frightened, she ordered Ribby to lock the door. 'Now,' she said to the little musician, 'you'll do as we say!' And she brought out a large orange-box and put it in the middle of the floor.

'Get in that box, quick sharp!' said the ogress. And the musician had to crawl inside, whether he liked it or not.

Then Wily Winnie said: 'You're to stay in that box and not make a sound until I give the box a kick. Then you must play "A Life on the Ocean Wave" on your concertina.'

'Do I have to sing as well?' asked the musician, whose knees were knocking together with fear.

'Certainly,' said Wily Winnie. 'What's more, you've to make up a song about Gapy Gob and me this instant

—something about how I love him and would like him to marry me.'

The musician thought as quickly as he could, and then he sang this song:

'Gapy Gob is bright and fair,
Combing down his yellow hair,
He's my ain for ever mair,
Bonny Gapy Gob—o!'

'Not my own idea, I'm afraid,' said the musician, 'but it's rather difficult to make up songs sitting in an orange-box.'

'It'll do,' said Wily Winnie. Then she sent the cat to fetch Gapy Gob, and smartened herself up as well as she could. Suddenly she remembered she would have to have a concertina herself, or Gapy Gob would never believe she was playing it.

'I must have a concertina,' she said.

'You'll find an old broken one in my sack,' said the musician. 'It hasn't a note in it.'

'Good,' said Wily Winnie. So she sat down and waited for Ribby to come back with Gapy Gob. But they were a very long time.

'I think I shall have to go and see what has happened to my cat,' said the ogress. 'You wait there.' And she left the musician sitting in the box. He hadn't been there long, however, before the door opened. Can you guess who came in? Katie Cook and Charlie Chop.

When the cat had arrived to invite Gapy Gob to come and listen to Wily Winnie playing the concertina, the children were quite sure something was up. So they had slipped out the back way and taken a short cut through the forest to the ogress's house. They had just seen Wily Winnie leave so they knew it was safe to go in.

'I wonder what's in that orange-box?' said Charlie Chop.

'It's me!' said the musician, and he told the children the whole story of what had happened to him after he had got lost.

'I'll show you the way home,' said Katie, 'but we'll have to be quick; the others will be here any moment now. Follow me!'

The musician crawled out of the box and ran out of the house with Katie as fast as his thin legs could carry him.

Charlie had borrowed the good concertina; now he crept into the box in the musician's place.

After a time the cat came back with Wily Winnie and Gapy Gob. The ogress was in high spirits. 'Now you just listen, Gapy Gob,' she said. 'I'm going to sit on this orange-box and play "A Life on the Ocean Wave" and you'll be *amazed*.' She picked up the old broken concertina, gave the box a kick, and started pretending to play.

But what came out was *not* 'A Life on the Ocean Wave' because, of course, it was Charlie Chop who was inside the box, and he made the most horrible noise he could on the concertina.

'Oh no, please stop!' said Gapy Gob, holding his ears. 'That was the most frightful noise I ever heard!'

'Perhaps you would like me to sing for you instead,' said Wily Winnie, and gave the box another kick. This was the signal for the musician to sing his song about Gapy Gob—you know, the one that went like 'Bobby Shaftoe':

> 'Gapy Gob is bright and fair,
> Combing down his yellow hair,
> He's my ain for ever mair,
> Bonny Gapy Gob—o!'

But this is what Charlie sang instead:

'Gapy is the ugliest fellow,
Ever since I first could bellow,
I have wished he was a toad
So I could chase him down the road.'

'Well!' said Gapy Gob. 'I must say! If you've brought me all this way to make a fool of me, I'll go home this minute, and that's flat! Toad, indeed!' And with that he stumped out of the house, slamming the door behind him.

'Wait, Gapy! Dear Gapy! I can explain!' wailed the ogress as she hurried after him. Charlie Chop took this chance to get out of the box and run home by the short cut.

All this time Ribby Ratsoup had been in the kitchen cooking a celebration feast for his mistress and Gapy Gob. She couldn't understand why everything was so quiet suddenly, so she came in to have a look. There was nobody there. Not even in the orange-box, though she got inside it to make sure.

Just at that moment Wily Winnie came back; she was *not* in high spirits *now*. 'So it's you who's been sitting in there mocking me!' she shouted. 'You wait till I get my broom! I'll give you the hiding of your life!'

Late that night, when the little musician had long since reached home, and Gapy Gob had had his supper, and Katie Cook and Charlie Chop had finished all their work for the day, two dark figures could be seen leaping from hill-top to hill-top; it was Wily Winnie chasing Ribby Ratsoup with her broom.

A birthday party in Topsy Turvy Town

In Topsy Turvy Town, where the sun rises in the West and goes down in the North, and three times fourteen is four, the Mayor was going to have his fiftieth birthday. His little girl, Trixie, was busy baking cakes, but she couldn't get on, because the Mayor *would* keep bothering her to know how much longer it would be before his birthday.

'Do stop bothering me, Daddy dear,' she said. 'When you've slept one more night it will be your birthday. So run along to your office now, please, and write out invitations to the people you want to come to your party.'

'I won't ask the Postmaster, anyway,' said the Mayor.

'Why ever not?'

'He always teases me about my big ears,' answered the Mayor.

'That's only when he's with the Smith,' said Trixie. 'You always play perfectly well when the Smith isn't there.'

'But I want to ask the Smith,' said the Mayor. 'I'm sure he'll behave if he knows we're having birthday cake.'

'Well, you'd better ask them both, then.'

'I want to ask the Doctor and the Dentist as well,' said the Mayor.

'I only hope the Doctor will be well enough to go out,' said Trixie. 'I spoke to his little girl yesterday, and she

told me he had had a very bad night, tossing and turning. She was afraid he might be sickening for something. But I expect you'd better ask him all the same.'

'Oh yes, otherwise he'd sulk,' said the Mayor. 'So would the Dentist.'

'You do as you like,' said Trixie, 'but you know he isn't allowed any sweet things like chocolate cake with icing on.'

'I know. But we could give him apples and rusks instead,' said the Mayor.

'That's a good idea. Are you asking any more?'

'What a question! I can't leave the Baker out, can I?'

'Now, now, that's not the way for a Mayor to talk to his little girl!' said Trixie. 'Anyway, if you ask him you can't have any more; there isn't room.' Then she told him to put the invitations through the letter-boxes and come straight home to bed to have a good sleep before the great day.

The next day the Mayor was very excited. He sat in his office and looked at the clock till it was time to go home. Then he raced back to put on his Grand Chain of Office and went and stood by the door to welcome his guests.

The first to arrive was the Smith. He had his hands in his pockets.

'Many Happy Returns of the Day,' he said.

'Thank you,' said the Mayor, holding out his hand for the present.

'Haven't brought a present,' said the Smith.

'Never mind,' said Trixie soothingly. 'Wouldn't you like to take off those big heavy boots before you come in?'

'No,' said the Smith.

'Why not?' asked the little girl.

'Hole in my sock,' said the Smith.

'You can borrow my daddy's slippers. And then what about taking your hands out of your pockets?'

'No,' said the Smith.

'Why not?'

'Dirty,' said the Smith.

'Oh, we'll soon deal with that!' said Trixie. 'You come along to the bathroom with me; I'll help you

wash them. You'll have to let the others in by yourself, Daddy dear.'

Next came the Doctor and the Dentist. They walked hand-in-hand and each had a little parcel under his arm.

'Many Happy Returns,' they said, both together.

'Thank you very much,' said the Mayor, and started

unwrapping. The Doctor's present was a stethoscope, but it was only a toy, because it was broken. The Dentist gave him a nice thing to squirt his mouth with.

Then came the Postmaster, and he brought a packet

of stamps which were very unusual, because all the edges had been cut off.

Last of all came the Baker. He brought a large slab of chocolate, and when he had wished the Mayor many happy returns he broke the chocolate in two, gave one half to the Mayor and stuffed the other half in his pocket.

'Come in, all of you,' Trixie said, as she came out of the bathroom with the Smith. His hands were now so clean, he was ashamed to show them.

In the dining-room there was a fine spread, with a huge birthday cake in the middle of the table decorated with fifty candles.

'Now do sit down and help yourselves,' invited Trixie. 'I'm just going to telephone.' And she shut the door. She picked up the receiver. 'Hullo, can you please give me the little girl in Flat 2?'

'There you are,' said the operator.

'Hullo, is that you, Kitty? This is Trixie.'

'Oh, hullo Trixie! What do you want?'

'Could you come and help me this afternoon? My daddy is having a birthday party and there *is* so much to do!'

'Yes, all right. But I'll have to bring my doll's ironing; there's a whole heap of it,' said Kitty on the telephone.

'We can iron together, then. *I* have a whole heap to do as well,' said Trixie.

As she put the 'phone down, Trixie heard a terrible crash from the dining-room, and when she opened the door what a sight met her eyes! There was birthday cake plastered all over the walls, and cups and saucers were strewn about the floor!

'What is the meaning of this?' she demanded sternly.

It was the Postmaster who answered. 'Well, you see, the Mayor tried to blow out the candles and he couldn't do it, so we all had a go and none of us could do it. Except the Smith.'

Trixie frowned. 'How did *you* manage it when the others couldn't do it?' she asked.

'Had my bellows,' said the Smith, staring up at the ceiling.

'Oh dear,' sighed Trixie. 'I suppose I shall have to clean up the mess. But then you really must behave. I have someone coming to see me, and we shall be in the nursery. So you're not to come in there. You can play in the sitting-room when you have finished your tea.' Then she left them to get on with it.

Trixie and her friend Kitty were ironing their dolls' clothes and having a very interesting talk together when suddenly there was another awful crash from the room where the party was going on. The Mayor came and knocked on the nursery door.

'What is it?' asked Trixie.

'It's the Postmaster,' said the Mayor; 'he's started teasing me again; I want him to go home.'

Trixie had to go and make peace. 'I really don't know why you can't play nicely instead of quarrelling,' she said.

The Postmaster was standing next to the Smith, staring at the floor. The Smith was looking at the ceiling, as usual.

'What did the Postmaster say?' asked Trixie.

'He said my ears were so big he would put a stamp on my forehead and send me by air-mail,' said the Mayor.

'*We* never put stamps on people and send them by air-mail,' said the Doctor and the Dentist, both together.

'Oh, how silly!' said Trixie. 'Now please be good boys and play a game, or something. What about Blind Man's Buff? Then I'll go and cook some lovely hot sausages for you.'

Trixie called to Kitty. 'I'll have to stop ironing dolls' clothes now, I must cook the sausages.'

'I'll come and help you,' said Kitty. 'I've finished my ironing.'

'Good,' said Trixie. But no sooner had they got to work in the kitchen than the door of the sitting-room flew open, and the Baker rushed out, grabbing his coat from the peg. Then he shot through the front door and down the main stairs, taking two at a time.

'*Now* what's happened?' asked Trixie.

The Mayor, who was nearly crying, came out in the kitchen. 'The Baker snatched his present back and ran off, just because he couldn't catch any of us in Blind Man's Buff,' he said.

'Oh dear! Oh dear!' said Trixie.

'*We* don't snatch our presents back and run off home,' said the Doctor and the Dentist.

'Of course not. You're *good* boys,' said Trixie, 'and I have some nice hot sausages for you.' Suddenly she noticed the Dentist's face. 'Goodness Gracious!' she exclaimed. 'What's that swelling you have on your cheek?' She beckoned to Kitty to have a look. 'I do believe he's got an ab—ab—what's it called?'

'You mean an abscess,' said Kitty, who was very clever. She climbed on the Dentist's knee. The Dentist opened his mouth wide, and, sure enough, he had an abscess!

'You'll have to go home to your little girl at once,' said Trixie, 'and get her to pull out the tooth for you.'

'He's not the only one who'll have to go home,' said Kitty. 'Look at the Doctor, he's coming out in spots all over his face. I expect he's getting measles.'

'Goodness Gracious!' cried Trixie. 'You'll all have to go at once before you catch the measles. Hurry and get your things on!'

So they all put on their coats and shook hands and said 'thank you' before they went home.

All except the Smith. He sat in the hall and took a very long time to put on his boots.

'You must go home to *your* little girl now,' said Trixie.

'Haven't got one,' said the Smith, with his eyes on the ceiling.

Trixie and Kitty both said 'Oh, you poor thing!' and they gave him all that was left of the birthday cake and a bucket, full of sausages, to take home.

The Mayor walked round the dining-room table, scraping all the plates and drinking all the cold tea. He thought it had been a wonderful party.

Father Christmas and the carpenter

THERE was once a carpenter called Anderson. He was a good father and he had a lot of children.

One Christmas Eve, while his wife and children were decorating the Christmas tree, Anderson crept out to his wood-shed. He had a surprise for them all: he was going to dress up as Father Christmas, load a sack of presents on to his sledge and go and knock on the front door. But as he pulled the loaded sledge out of the wood-shed, he slipped and fell right across the sack of presents. This set the sledge moving, because the ground sloped from the shed down to the road, and Anderson had no time even to shout 'Way there!' before he crashed into another sledge which was coming down the road.

'I'm very sorry,' said Anderson.

'Don't mention it; I couldn't stop myself,' said the other man. Like Anderson, he was dressed in Father Christmas clothes and had a sack on his sledge.

'We seem to have had the same idea,' said Anderson. 'I see you're all dressed up like me.' He laughed and shook the other man's hand. 'My name's Anderson.'

'Glad to meet you,' said the other. 'I'm Father Christmas.'

'Ha, ha!' laughed Anderson. 'You will have your little joke, and quite right too on a Christmas Eve.'

'That's what I thought,' said the other man, 'and if you agree we can change places tonight, and that will be a better joke still; I'll take the presents along to *your* children, if you'll go and visit *mine*. But you must take off that costume.'

Anderson looked a bit puzzled. 'What am I to dress up in then?'

'You don't need to dress up at all,' said the other. 'My children see Father Christmas all the year round, but they've never seen a real carpenter. I told them last Christmas that if they were good this year I'd try and get the carpenter to come and see them while I went round with presents for the human children.'

'So he really *is* Father Christmas,' thought Anderson to himself. Out loud he said: 'All right, if you really want me to, I will. The only thing is, I haven't any presents for your children.'

'Presents?' said Father Christmas. 'Aren't you a carpenter?'

'Yes, of course.'

'Well, then, all you have to do is to take along a few pieces of wood and some nails. You have a knife, I suppose?' Anderson said he had and went to look for the things in his workshop.

'Just follow my footsteps in the snow; they'll lead you to my house in the forest,' said Father Christmas. 'Then I'll take your sack and sledge and go and knock on your door.

'Righto!' said the carpenter.

Then Father Christmas went off to knock at Anderson's door, and the carpenter trudged through the snow in Father Christmas's footsteps. They led him into the forest, past two pine-trees, a large boulder and a tree-stump. There, peeping out from behind the stump, were three little faces with red caps on.

'He's here! He's here!' shouted the Christmas children as they scampered in front of him to a fallen tree, lying with its roots in the air. When Anderson followed them round to the other side of the roots he found Mother Christmas standing there waiting for him.

'Here he is, Mum! Here's the carpenter Dad promised us! Look at him! Isn't he tall!' The children were all shouting at once.

'Now, now, children,' said Mother Christmas, 'anybody would think you'd never seen a human being before.'

'We've never seen a proper *carpenter* before!' shouted the children. 'Come on in, Mr. Carpenter!'

Pulling a branch aside, Mother Christmas led the way into the house. Anderson had to bend his long back double and crawl on his hands and knees. But once in, he found he could straighten up. The room had a mud floor, but it was very cosy, with tree-stumps for chairs, and beds made of moss with covers of plaited grass. In the smallest bed lay the Christmas baby and in the far corner sat a very old Grandfather Christmas, his red cap nodding up and down.

'Have you got a knife? Did you bring some wood and some nails?' The children wanted to know everything at once and pulled at Anderson's sleeve.

'Now, children,' said Mother Christmas, 'let the carpenter sit down before you start pestering him.'

'Has anyone come to see me?' croaked old Grandfather Christmas.

Mother Christmas shouted in his ear. 'It's Anderson, the carpenter!' She explained that Grandfather was so old he never went out any more. 'He'd be pleased if you came over and shook hands with him.'

So Anderson took the old man's hand which was as hard as a piece of bark.

'Come and sit here, Mr. Carpenter!' called the children.

The eldest one spoke first. 'D'you know what I want you to make for me? A toboggan. Can you do that—a little one, I mean?'

'I'll try,' said Anderson, and it didn't take long before he had a smart toboggan just ready to fly over the snow.

'Now it's my turn,' said the little girl who had pigtails sticking straight out from her head. 'I want a doll's bed.'

'Have you any dolls?' asked Anderson.

'No, but I borrow the field-mice sometimes, and I can play with the baby squirrels as much as I like. They *love* being dolls. Please make me a doll's bed.'

So the carpenter made her a doll's bed. Then he asked the smaller boy what he would like. But he was very shy and could only whisper, 'Don't know.'

' 'Course he knows!' said his sister. 'He said it just before you came. Go on, tell the carpenter.'

'A top,' whispered the little boy.

'That's easy,' said the carpenter, and in no time at all he had made a top.

'And now you must make something for Mum!' said the children. Mother Christmas had been watching, but all the time she held something behind her back.

'Shush, children, don't keep bothering the carpenter,' she said.

'That's all right,' said Anderson. 'What would you like me to make?'

Mother Christmas brought out the thing she was holding; it was a wooden ladle, very worn, with a crack in it.

'Could you mend this for me, d'you think?' she asked.

'Hm, hm!' said Anderson, scratching his ear with his carpenter's pencil. 'I think I'd better make you a new one.' And he quickly cut a new ladle for Mother Christmas. Then he found a long twisted root with a crook at

one end and started stripping it with his knife. But, although the children asked him and asked him, he wouldn't tell them what it was going to be. When it was finished he held it up; it was a very distinguished-looking walking-stick.

'Here you are, Grandpa!' he shouted to the old man, and handed him the stick. Then he gathered up all the chips and made a wonderful little bird with wings outspread to hang over the baby's cot.

'How pretty!' exclaimed Mother Christmas and all the children. 'Thank the carpenter nicely now. We'll certainly never forget this Christmas Eve, will we?'

'Thank you, Mr. Carpenter, thank you very much!' shouted the children.

Grandfather Christmas himself came stumping across the room, leaning on his new stick. 'It's grand!' he said. 'It's just grand!'

There was a sound of feet stamping the snow off outside the door, and Anderson knew it was time for him to go. He said goodbye all round and wished them a Happy Christmas. Then he crawled through the narrow opening under the fallen tree. Father Christmas was waiting for him. He had the sledge and the empty sack with him.

'Thank you for your help, Anderson,' he said. 'What did the youngsters say when they saw you?'

'Oh, they seemed very pleased. Now they're just waiting for you to come home and see their new toys. How did you get on at my house? Was little Peter frightened of you?'

'Not a bit,' said Father Christmas. 'He thought I was you. "Sit on Dadda's knee," he kept saying.'

'Well, I must get back to them,' said Anderson, and said goodbye to Father Christmas.

When he got home, the first thing he said to the children was, 'Can I see the presents you got from Father Christmas?'

But the children laughed. 'Silly! You've seen them already—when you were Father Christmas; you unpacked them all for us!'

'What would you say if I told you I had been with Father Christmas's family all this time?'

But the children laughed again. 'You wouldn't say anything so silly!' they said, and they didn't believe him. So the carpenter came to me and asked me to write the story down, which I did.

Mrs Pepperpot to the Rescue
and other stories

MRS PEPPERPOT

to the Rescue

and other stories by

ALF PRØYSEN

Translated by Marianne Helweg

Illustrated by Björn Berg

Contents

Mrs Pepperpot to the Rescue

and other stories

Mrs Peppercpot to the Rescue

WHEN IT IS breaking-up day at the village school, and the summer holidays are about to begin, all the children bring flowers to decorate the school. They pick them in their own gardens or they get them from their uncles and aunts, and then they carry their big bunches along the road, while they sing and shout because it is the end of term. Their mothers and fathers wave to them from the windows and wish them a happy breaking-up day.

But in one window stands a little old woman who just watches the children go by. That is Mrs Pepperpot.

She has no one now to wish a happy breaking-up day, for all her own children are long since grown up and gone away, and none of the young ones think of asking her for flowers.

At least, that's not quite true; I do know of one little girl who picked flowers in Mrs Pepperpot's garden. But that was several years ago, not long after the little old woman first started shrinking to the size of a pepperpot at the most inconvenient moments.

That particular summer Mrs Pepperpot's garden was fairly bursting with flowers: there were white lilac with boughs almost laden to the ground, blue and red anemones on strong, straight stalks, poppies with graceful nodding yellow heads and many other lovely flowers. But no one had asked Mrs Pepperpot for any of them, so she just stood in her window and watched as the children went by, singing and shouting, on their way to the breaking-up day at school.

The very last to cross the yard in front of her house was a little girl, and she was walking, oh, so slowly, and

carried nothing in her hands. Mrs Pepperpot's cat was lying on the doorstep and greeted her with a 'Miaow!' But the little girl only made a face and said, 'Stupid animal!' And when Mrs Pepperpot's dog, which was chained to the wall, started barking and wagging his tail the little girl snapped, 'Hold your tongue!'

Then Mrs Pepperpot opened the window to throw a bone out to the dog and the little girl whirled round and shouted angrily, 'Don't you throw that dirty bone on my dress!'

That was enough. Mrs Pepperpot put her hands on her hips and told the little girl that no one had any right to cross the yard in front of her house and throw insulting words at her or her cat and dog, which were doing no harm to anybody.

The little girl began to cry. 'I want to go home,' she sobbed. 'I've an awful pain in my tummy and I don't want to go to the breaking-up party! Why should I go when I have a pain in my tummy?'

'Where's your mother, child?' asked Mrs Pepperpot.

'None of your business!' snapped the girl.

'Well, where's your father, then?' asked Mrs Pepperpot.

'Never you mind!' said the girl, still more rudely. 'But if you want to know why I don't want to go to school today it's because I haven't any flowers. We haven't a garden, anyway, as we've only been here since Christmas. But Dad's going to build us a house now that he's working at the ironworks, and then we'll have a garden. My mum makes paper flowers and does the paper round, see? Anything more you'd like to know? Oh well, I might as well go to school, I suppose. Teacher can say what she likes—I don't care! If *she'd* been going from school to school for three years she wouldn't know much either! So blow her and her flowers!' And the little girl stared defiantly at Mrs Pepperpot.

Mrs Pepperpot stared back at the little girl and then

she said: 'That's the spirit! But I think I can help you with the flowers. Just you go out in the garden and pick some lilac and anemones and poppies and anything else you like. I'll go and find some paper for you to wrap them in.'

So the girl went into the garden and started picking flowers while Mrs Pepperpot went indoors for some paper. But just as she was coming back to the door she shrank!

Roly Poly! And there she was, tucked up in the paper like jam in a pudding, when the little girl came running back with her arms full of flowers.

'Here we are!' shouted the little girl.

'And here *we* are!' said Mrs Pepperpot as she disentangled herself from the paper. 'Don't be scared; this is something that happens to me from time to time, and I never know when I'm going to shrink. But now I've got an idea; I want you to pop me in your satchel and take me along with you to school. We're going to have a game with them all! What's your name, by the way?'

'It's Rita,' said the little girl who was staring at Mrs Pepperpot with open mouth.

'Well, Rita, don't just stand there. Hurry up and put the paper round those flowers. There's no time to lose!'

When they got to the school the breaking-up party was well under way, and the teacher didn't look particularly pleased even when Rita handed her the lovely bunch of flowers. She just nodded and said, 'Thanks.'

'Take no notice,' said Mrs Pepperpot from Rita's satchel.

'Go to your desk,' said the teacher. Rita sat down with her satchel on her knee.

'We'll start with a little arithmetic,' said the teacher. 'What are seven times seven?'

'Forty-nine!' whispered Mrs Pepperpot from the satchel.

'Forty-nine!' said Rita.

This made the whole class turn round and stare at Rita, for up to now she had hardly been able to count to thirty! But Rita stared back at them and smiled. Then she stole a quick look at her satchel.

'What's that on your lap?' asked the teacher. 'Nobody is allowed to use a crib. Give me your satchel at once!'

So Rita had to carry it up to the teacher's desk where it was hung on a peg.

The teacher went on to the next question: 'If we take fifteen from eighteen what do we get?'

All the children started counting on their fingers, but Rita saw that Mrs Pepperpot was sticking both her arms and one leg out of the satchel.

'Three!' said Rita before the others had had time to answer.

This time nobody suspected her of cheating and Rita beamed all over while Mrs Pepperpot waved to her from between the pages of her exercise book.

'Very strange, I must say,' said the teacher. 'Now we'll have a little history and geography. Which country is it that has a long wall running round it and has the oldest culture in the world?'

Rita was watching the satchel the whole time, and now she saw Mrs Pepperpot's head pop up again. The little old woman had smeared her face with yellow chalk and now she put her fingers in the corners of her eyes and pulled them into narrow slits.

'China!' shouted Rita.

The teacher was quite amazed at this answer, but she had to admit that Rita was right. Then she made an announcement.

'Children,' she said, 'I have decided to award a treat to the one of you who gave the most right answers. Rita gave me all the right answers, so she is the winner, and she will be allowed to serve coffee to the teachers in the staff-room afterwards.'

Rita felt very pleased and proud; she was so used to getting meals ready when she was alone at home that she was sure she could manage this all right. So, when the other children went home, she took her satchel from the teacher's desk and went out into the kitchen. But, oh dear, it wasn't a bit like home! The coffee-pot was far too big and the huge cake with icing on it was very different from the plate of bread-and-dripping she usually got ready for her parents at home. Luckily the cups and saucers and plates and spoons had all been laid out on the table beforehand. All the same, it seemed too much to Rita, and she just sat down and cried. In a moment she heard the sound of scratching from the satchel, and out stepped Mrs Pepperpot.

'If you're the girl I take you for,' said the little old woman, putting her hands on her hips, 'you won't give up half-way like this! Come on, just you lift me up on the table, we'll soon have this job done! As far as I could see from my hiding place, there are nine visiting teachers and your own Miss Snooty. That makes two cups of water and two dessertspoons of coffee per person—which makes twenty cups of water and twenty dessertspoons of coffee in all—right?'

'I think so. Oh, you're wonderful!' said Rita, drying her tears. 'I'll measure out the water and coffee at once, but I don't know how I'm going to cut up that cake!'

'That'll be all right,' said Mrs. Pepperpot. 'As far as I can see the cake is about ninety paces—my paces—round. So if we divide it by ten that'll make each piece nine paces. But that will be too big for each slice, so we'll divide nine by three and make each piece three paces thick. Right?'

'I expect so,' said Rita, who was getting a bit lost.

'But first we must mark a circle in the middle of the cake,' went on Mrs Pepperpot. 'Lift me up on your hand, please.'

Rita lifted her carefully on to her hand.

'Now take me by the legs and turn me upside down. Then, while you swing me round, I can mark a circle with one finger in the icing. Right; let's go!'

So Rita swung Mrs Pepperpot round upside down and the result was a perfect little circle drawn right in the middle of the cake.

'Crumbs are better than no bread!' said Mrs Pepperpot as she stood there, swaying giddily and licking her finger. 'Now I'll walk right round the cake, and at every third step I want you to make a little notch in the icing with the knife. Here we go!

'One, two, three, notch!
One, two, three, notch!
One, two, three, notch!'

And in this way Mrs Pepperpot marched all round the cake, and Rita notched it so that it made exactly thirty slices when it was cut.

When they had finished someone called from the staff-room: 'Where's that clever girl with the coffee? Hurry up and bring it in, dear, then you can fetch the cake afterwards.'

Rita snatched up the big coffee-pot, which was boiling now, and hurried in with it, and Mrs Pepperpot stood listening to the way the teachers praised Rita as she poured the coffee into the cups with a steady hand.

After a while she came out for the cake. Mrs Pepperpot clapped her hands: 'Well done, Rita! There's nothing to worry about now.'

But she shouldn't have said that, for while she was listening to the teachers telling Rita again how clever she was, she suddenly heard that Miss Snooty raising her voice:

'I'm afraid you've forgotten two things, dear,' she said.

'Oh dear!' thought Mrs Pepperpot, 'the cream-jug and the sugar-bowl! I shall have to look and see if they are both filled.'

The cream-jug was full, but when Mrs Pepperpot leaned over the edge of the sugar-bowl she toppled in! And at the same moment Rita rushed in, put the lid on the sugar-bowl and put it and the cream-jug on a little tray. Then she turned round and went back to the staff-room.

First Mrs Pepperpot wondered if she should tell Rita where she was, but she was afraid the child might drop the tray altogether, so instead she buried herself well down in the sugar-bowl and hoped for the best.

Rita started carrying the tray round. But her teacher hadn't finished with her yet. 'I hope you remembered the sugar-tongs,' she said.

Rita didn't know what to say, but Mrs Pepperpot heard the remark, and when the visiting head teacher took the lid off, Mrs Pepperpot popped up like a jack-in-the-box holding a lump of sugar in her outstretched hand. She stared straight in front of her and never moved

an eyelid, so the head teacher didn't notice anything odd. He simply took the sugar lump and waved Rita on with the tray. But his neighbour at the table looked hard at Mrs Pepperpot and said: 'What very curious sugar-tongs—I suppose they're made of plastic. Whatever will they think of next?' Then he asked Rita if she had brought them with her from home, and she said yes, which was strictly true, of course.

After that everyone wanted to have a look at the curious sugar-tongs, till in the end Rita's teacher called her over.

'Let me have a look at those tongs,' she said. She reached out her hand to pick them up, but this was too much for Mrs Pepperpot. In a moment she had the whole tray over and everything fell on the floor. The

cream-jug was smashed and the contents of the sugar-bowl rolled under the cupboard, which was just as well for Mrs Pepperpot!

But the teacher thought it was she who had upset the tray, and suddenly she was sorry she had been so hard on the little girl. She put her arms round Rita and gave her a hug. 'It was all my fault,' she said. 'You've been a very good little parlourmaid.'

Later, when all the guests had gone, and Rita was clearing the table, the teacher pointed to the dark corner by the cupboard and said, 'Who is that standing there?'

And out stepped Mrs Pepperpot as large as life and quite unruffled. 'I've been sent to lend a hand with the washing-up,' she said. 'Give me that tray, Rita. You and I will go out into the kitchen.'

When at last the two of them were walking home, Rita said, 'Why did you help me all day when I was so horrid to you this morning?'

'Well,' said Mrs Pepperpot, 'perhaps it was because you *were* so horrid. Next time maybe I'll help that Miss Snooty of yours. She looks pretty horrid too, but she might be nice underneath.'

Mrs Pepperpot on the Warpath

IT WAS the day after Mrs Pepperpot had helped Rita at the school party, and the little old woman was in a terrible rage. You see, if there's anything Mrs Pepperpot hates, it's people being unkind to children. All night she had been thinking about it, and now she had made up her mind to go and tell Rita's teacher just what she thought of her. So she put on her best hat and her best frock, straightened her back and marched off to the school.

'I hope I don't shrink this time,' she thought, 'but it's not likely to happen two days running. Anyway, today I must have my say or I shall burst. Somebody's going to say she's sorry or my name's not Pepperpot!'

She had reached the school gate and swung it open. Then she walked up to the teacher's front door and knocked twice smartly. Then she waited.

No one said, 'Come in!'

Mrs Pepperpot knocked again, but there was still no answer. So she decided to try the latch. 'If the door isn't locked I shall go straight in,' she said to herself. She pressed the latch and the door opened. But no sooner had she put a foot over the threshold than she shrank and fell head over heels into a travelling-rug which was rolled up on the floor just inside the door! Next to it stood a suitcase and a hatbox.

'Oh, calamity!' cried Mrs Pepperpot, 'let's hope she's not in after all now!' But she was unlucky, for now she could hear footsteps in the corridor and the teacher came towards the front door dressed in her going-out clothes.

'What an old dolt I am!' thought Mrs Pepperpot. 'Fancy me not remembering the summer holidays have started today and she'll be going away, of course. Oh well, she's not gone yet. If I can manage to stay near her

for a little while longer I may still get my chance to give her a piece of my mind.' So she hid in the rug.

The teacher picked up the suitcase in one hand, then she threw the travelling-rug over her shoulder and picked up the hatbox in the other hand and walked out of the house, closing the door behind her. And Mrs Pepperpot? She was clinging for dear life to the fringe of the rug and she was still as angry as ever.

'Very nice, I must say!' she muttered. 'Going away on a holiday like this without a thought for Rita and all the harm you did her. But you wait, my fine lady, very soon it'll be my turn to teach you a thing or two!'

The teacher walked briskly on, with Mrs Pepperpot dangling behind her, till they got to the station. Then she walked over to the fruit-stall and put the rug down on the counter, and Mrs Pepperpot was able to slip out of it and hide behind a bunch of flowers.

The teacher asked for two pounds of apples.

'That's right!' fumed Mrs Pepperpot to herself. 'Buy two pounds of apples to gorge yourself with on the train!'

'And eight oranges, please,' continued the teacher.

'Worse and worse!' muttered Mrs Pepperpot.

'And three pounds of bananas, please,' said the teacher.

Mrs Pepperpot could hardly contain herself: 'If I was my proper size now, I'd give you apples and oranges and bananas, and no mistake!'

Then the teacher said to the lady in the fruit-stall:

'Do you think you could do me a favour? I want all this fruit to go to one of my pupils, but I have to catch the train, so I've no time to take it to her myself. Could you deliver it to Rita Johansen in the little house by the church and tell her it's from me?'

On hearing this, Mrs Pepperpot's ears nearly fell off with astonishment. It was just as if someone had taken a sweet out of her mouth and left her nothing to suck; what was she going to say now?

'I'll do that for you with pleasure, miss,' said the fruit-lady. 'That'll be twelve shillings exactly.'

'Oh dear!' exclaimed the teacher, rummaging in her purse, 'I see I shan't have enough money left after buying my ticket. Would you mind if I owed you the twelve shillings till I come back from my holidays?'

'The very idea! Asking me to deliver goods you can't

even pay for! I shall have to have the fruit back, please,' the fruit-lady said, and held out her hand.

The teacher said she was sorry, put the bag of fruit back on the counter and went off to board her train, but Mrs Pepperpot had taken the chance to jump into the bag.

Silently she wished the teacher a good holiday: 'You're not so bad after all, and you needn't worry; I'll see that Rita gets her bag of fruit somehow. But *somebody*'s going to get the edge of my tongue before the day's out!'

Of course the fruit-lady could no more hear what Mrs Pepperpot was saying than the teacher could. She was busy getting ready to shut up shop and go home. But when she had put her hat on and opened the door she suddenly turned round and picked up the bag of fruit on the counter.

Mrs Pepperpot had just been wondering if she was going to be locked in the fruit-stall all night, and now here she was, being taken on another journey!

'I suppose you're going to eat all this yourself, you selfish old thing, you!' thought Mrs Pepperpot, getting worked up again. 'The teacher may be snooty, but at least she has a kind heart underneath. You're just plain mean! But just you wait till I grow again!'

The fruit-lady walked on and on, until at last Mrs

Pepperpot could hear her opening a door and going into a room. There she set the bag down with a thump on the table, and Mrs Pepperpot was able to climb over an orange and peep out of the top.

She saw a man banging on the table, and he was as cross as a sore bear. 'What sort of time is this to come home?' he roared. 'I've been waiting and waiting for my supper. Hurry up now! What's in that bag, anyway?'

'Oh, it's only some fruit for a little girl,' said his wife. 'The school-teacher wanted to send it to Rita Johansen, but she found she hadn't enough money, so I took it back. Then when she'd gone I felt sorry, so I thought I'd take it along to the child myself.'

This time Mrs Pepperpot was really amazed: 'Well, I never!' she gasped, 'here's another one who turns out to be nice. Still, I'm sure her husband won't; he looks as if he could do with a good ticking off!'

The fruit-lady's husband certainly was a cross-patch and no mistake. He banged his fist on the table and shouted that no wife of his was going to waste money and time running errands for silly school-teachers and brats.

'Give me that bag!' he roared. 'I'll take it right back to the shop this minute!' And he snatched up the bag from the table. Poor Mrs Pepperpot was given an awful shaking and landed up jammed between two bananas.

Taking long strides, the man walked off down the road.

'Bye-bye, fruit-lady!' whispered Mrs Pepperpot. 'You have a nasty husband, but I'll deal with him shortly, don't you worry!'

Squeezed and bruised, the little old woman lay there in the bag while the man strode on. But after a while he walked more slowly and at last he stopped at a house and knocked on the door.

'Surely this isn't the station?' wondered Mrs Pepperpot.

She heard the door open and the man spoke: 'Are you Rita Johansen?'

Then she heard a little girl's voice, 'Yes, that's me.'

'Your teacher sent you this,' said the man and handed over the bag; 'it's fruit.'

'Oh, thank you!' said Rita. 'I'll just go and get a bowl to put it in.' And she set the bag on a chair.

'That's all right,' said the man, and he turned on his heel and walked away.

When Rita came back with the bowl she thought she heard the door close, but she didn't take much notice in her eagerness to see what the teacher had sent her.

But it was actually Mrs Pepperpot who had slipped out, for she was now her usual size and she wanted time to think; it had all been so surprising and not at all what she expected. As she walked she began to hurry. For now she knew who was going to get a piece of her mind, and rightly so! Someone who made her more angry than anyone else just now!

When she got home she marched straight to the mirror. Putting her hands on her hips she glared at the little old woman she saw there. 'Well!' she said, 'and who do you think you are, running round the country-side, poking your nose in where you're not wanted? Is it any of your business, may I ask, who the school-teacher buys fruit for? What d'you mean by hiding in people's travelling-rugs and spying on them? You ought to be ashamed of yourself, an old woman like you, behaving like a senseless child. As for the fruit-lady, why shouldn't she be cross? How was she to know if she could trust the teacher? And her husband; I suppose he can bang his fist on his own table if he likes without you interfering? Are you listening? Wouldn't you be pretty mad if you'd come home hungry and the wife wasn't there to cook your meal, eh? I'm disgusted with you! *They* were sorry for what they did and made amends, all three of them, but *you*, you just stand there glaring at me as if nothing had happened. Wouldn't it be an idea to say you were sorry?'

Mrs Pepperpot turned her back on the mirror and took a deep breath. 'That's better!' she said. 'I've got it all off my chest at last. Now I can give my tongue a rest and get on with the housework.'

But first she took one more look in the mirror, smiled shyly and bobbed a little curtsy.

'I'm sorry!' she said.

And the little old woman in the mirror smiled back at her and bobbed a little curtsy too.

The Nature Lesson

EVERY MORNING, when Mrs Pepperpot sits at her window with her after-breakfast cup of coffee, she watches a little boy who always walks across her yard on his way to school. The boy's name is Olly and he and Mrs Pepperpot are very good friends, though not in the way grown-ups usually are friends with children. Quite often Olly rushes past Mrs Pepperpot's window without even saying 'Good morning', because he is in such a hurry. But then Mrs Pepperpot has never even asked him his name or how old he is or what he wants for Christmas. She just watches him every morning and says to herself, 'There goes the little boy on his way to school.' As for Olly, he just glances up at her window and thinks, 'There's the old woman, drinking her coffee.'

Now with animals it is different: if Olly sees the cat sitting on Mrs Pepperpot's door-step he can't resist stopping to stroke her. He'll even sit down on the door-step and talk to her.

'Hullo, pussy,' he'll say. 'There's a lovely pussy!' And then, of course, he has to go and see the dog outside his kennel as well, in case he should get jealous.

'Hullo, boy! Good dog, good dog! You didn't think I'd forgotten you, did you? Oh, I wouldn't do that! There's a good dog!' And by the time he's made a fuss of them both he's late for school.

This is Olly's trouble: he's *very* fond of animals. He loves to play hide-and-seek with the squirrel he sees on his way to school, or to have a whistling-match with a blackbird. And as for *rainy* days, well, he spends so much time trying not to step on the worms wriggling by the puddles in the road that he's *always* late for school.

This won't do, of course, and when he's late his teacher gets cross, and she'll say, 'It's all very well being fond of animals; it's quite right that you should be, but it's no excuse for being late for school.'

But that wasn't what I was going to tell you. What I was going to tell you was how Mrs Pepperpot had a nature lesson one day. So here we go!

It was a lovely spring day, and Mrs Pepperpot was sitting by the window as usual, enjoying her cup of coffee and watching Olly come across the yard. He was walking rather briskly this time—watching some bird or animal had probably made him late again—so he had

only time to say 'Hullo, puss!' to the cat on the door-step and 'Hi, boy!' to the dog by the kennel.

But suddenly he stopped dead, turned round on his heel and started running back across the yard. Mrs Pepperpot had just come to the door to give the dog his breakfast and Olly rushed past her as fast as he could go.

Mrs Pepperpot called to him: 'Whatever's the matter with you, boy? The police after you?'

'Forgot my nature textbook!' answered Olly over his shoulder, and started off again.

'Wait a minute!' called Mrs Pepperpot. Olly stopped. 'You can't go all the way home again now; you'll be much too late for school. No, you go on and *I'll* go back for your book and bring it to you at school.'

Olly shuffled his feet a bit and looked unhappy; he didn't much like the idea of an old woman turning up in school with his nature textbook.

'Don't stand there shuffling, boy!' said Mrs Pepperpot. 'Where did you leave the book?'

'On the window-sill,' he answered; 'the window is open.'

'All right. Where do you want me to put the book when I get to the school? Come on, hurry up; we haven't got all day!' said Mrs Pepperpot, trying to look severe.

'There's a hole in the wall, just by the big birch tree; there's an old bird-nest there you can put it in.'

'In the old nest in a hole in the wall by the birch tree; right!' said Mrs Pepperpot. 'Now, off you go and see if you can be on time for a change! I'll see to the rest.'

'Righto!' said Olly and was off before you could say Jack Robinson.

Mrs Pepperpot took off her apron, smoothed her hair and stepped out into the yard. And then, of course, the inevitable thing happened; she shrank!

'This is bad,' thought Mrs Pepperpot, as she peeped over the wet grass by the door-step, 'but I've known worse.' She called to the cat: 'Come here, puss! You'll have to be my horse once again and help me fetch Olly's nature book from his house.'

'Miaow! All right,' said the cat, as she allowed Mrs Pepperpot to climb on her back. 'What sort of a thing is a nature book?'

'It's a book the children use in school to learn about animals,' answered Mrs Pepperpot, 'and one thing it says about cats is that you are "carnivores".'

'What does that mean?' asked the cat.

'That you eat meat, but never mind that now; all you have to do is to take me straight down the road till we get to the stream. Then we take a short cut across. . . .'

But, as they came near the stream, the cat said, 'Doesn't the book say anything about cats not liking to get their feet wet?' And then she stopped so abruptly that poor Mrs Pepperpot toppled right over her head and fell plump into the water!

'Good job I can swim,' spluttered Mrs Pepperpot as she came to the surface, 'humans aren't meant to live under water on account of the way they breathe with their lungs. Phew! It's hard work all the same; I'll take a rest on this stone and see if something turns up.'

While she was getting her breath a tiny animal stuck its nose out of the water, and started snarling at her. Now Mrs Pepperpot knew what that was, but you probably wouldn't, because it only lives in the faraway places, and it is called a lemming. Its fur is dappled brown and fawn, so that it looks a bit like a guinea-pig in summer, but in winter it turns white as the snow around it.

As I say, Mrs Pepperpot knew all about lemmings, so she snarled back at the little creature, making as horrible a noise as she could. 'I'm not afraid of you!' she said, 'though the book says you're the worst-tempered of all the little rodents and don't give way to a fierce dog or even a grown man. But now you can just stop showing off and help me out of this stream like a good lemming.'

'Well, blow me down!' said the lemming. 'I never saw a woman as small as you and with such a loud voice. Get on my back and I'll take you across. Where are you going, by the way?'

'To fetch a nature book from the house over there for a little boy at school,' said Mrs Pepperpot. 'And in that book there is quite a bit about you.'

'Oh? And what does it say?' asked the lemming, crawling out on to the grass with Mrs Pepperpot.

'It says that once every so many years lemmings come down from the mountains in great swarms and eat up all the green stuff they can find till they get to the sea.' Then she stopped, because she remembered that when the lemmings reach the sea in their search for food, thousands of them get drowned.

'We do get rather hungry,' said the lemming; 'as a matter of fact, I'm on my way now to join my mates in a little food-hunt. . . .'

'Couldn't you just take me down to the house?' pleaded Mrs Pepperpot; she didn't like the idea that he might drown in the sea. But the lemming's empty tummy was telling him to go, so he told Mrs Pepperpot she would have to manage by herself, and he ran off muttering to himself about juicy green leaves.

Before Mrs Pepperpot had had time to wonder what

would happen to him, another head appeared above a little wall. This time it was a stoat.

'Hullo, Mr Nosey Parker,' she greeted him, 'what are you looking for?'

'I thought you were a mouse, but I see you're a little old woman, and I don't eat women,' said the stoat. 'Have you by any chance got a silver spoon?' he added.

'I have something you like even better than silver spoons,' answered Mrs Pepperpot, 'a whole packet of tin-tacks, and you can have them if you'll take me to that house over there. I have to fetch a book from the window-sill for a little boy in the school.'

'All right,' said the stoat, 'hop up!'

So Mrs Pepperpot got on his back. But it was a most

uncomfortable journey, because stoats, like weasels, move by rippling their long bodies, and though they have short legs, they can run very fast. Mrs Pepperpot had a job keeping on and was glad when they reached the wall under the window.

The stoat scrambled up to the window-sill, and presently he came back with the book—under his chin.

'Why do you carry the book that way?' asked Mrs Pepperpot.

'How else?' answered the stout. 'I always carry eggs under my chin.'

'Eggs?' Mrs Pepperpot pretended to be surprised. 'I didn't know stoats laid eggs.'

'Ha, ha, very funny!' said the stoat. 'I suppose you don't eat eggs?'

'Oh yes,' said Mrs Pepperpot, 'but I don't steal them out of wild birds' nests.'

'That's my business,' said the stoat. 'Now you'd better think how you're going to get this book to school; I can't carry both you and the book.'

'That's true!' said Mrs Pepperpot. 'I'll have to think of something.'

But it wasn't necessary, for the next moment Mrs Pepperpot was back to her proper size. As she bent down to pick up the book she whispered to the little stoat, 'The tin-tacks will be waiting for you in that nest you robbed in the stone wall by the school.' And she thought she heard him chuckle as he rippled away in the grass.

When she reached the school the bell was ringing for break, and she just had time to pop the book into the empty nest before Olly came running out with the other children. Mrs Pepperpot gave the tiniest nod in the direction of the wall and then she walked briskly away.

But the next morning Olly brought a lovely bone for her dog and from his milk bottle he poured a good saucer-full of milk for her pussy.

Mrs Pepperpot opened the window. 'Would you do something for me this morning?' she asked.

'As long as it won't make me late for school,' answered Olly.

'Good,' said Mrs Pepperpot. Then she fetched a packet of tin-tacks from the toolshed and gave them to Olly. 'Put those in the empty nest in the wall, will you? They're for a friend of mine.'

The Shoemaker's Doll

THERE WAS once a shoemaker who won a doll in a raffle at a bazaar. But a doll was no good to him, living alone as he did in a little cottage where the floor was strewn with old soles and bits of leather and where everything he touched was covered in glue.

For, with all the village shoemaking to be done before he could do his own housework, you can imagine what the shoemaker's home looked like. And now there was this doll. When he had brought it home he stood looking round the little room and wondering where on earth he could put it. At last he decided to set the doll on top of the chest of drawers next to a half-loaf of bread and a rubber boot. Then he went to bed.

In the night he dreamed that the doll came over to his bed and said:

> 'I can scrub, I can sweep,
> Make a bed and house-keep;
> If *you* won't, *I* will!'

When the shoemaker opened his eyes next morning and saw the doll on the chest of drawers he remembered the dream and laughed to himself.

'So you can scrub and sweep and make beds, can you, my little flibberty gibbett? Still, I suppose I had better do it myself to save you spoiling your pretty frock,' he said. So he made his bed, which hadn't been done properly for fifteen years, and underneath he found the old gold watch his grandfather had left him. Until that moment he thought it was lost for ever. After that he washed the floor and found a half-crown lying in a corner behind the cupboard. Then he swept out all the rubbish from the drawer in his work-bench, and what do you think?

Right at the bottom he found a little ring with a red stone in it!

At first the shoemaker was astonished, but then he remembered:

'Yes, yes, of course! It was that little girl from Crag House; she did tell me she had lost her ring here once. She came to ask me about it several times. I'll put it on the shelf here and give it to her when I see her. And now I suppose I'd better tidy up the chest of drawers for you, my little slave-driver!'

He started by removing the rubber boot. But he decided to leave the half-loaf, because he liked to take a bite from time to time while he was mending the shoes.

Later in the day a village woman came in. When she

saw how tidy the room was she clapped her hands and exclaimed: 'Well I never! What a change! You must have had a lot of time to spare getting the place so ship-shape. I suppose you have my shoes ready as well, then?'

The shoemaker pushed his spectacles up on his forehead and stared at the woman. Then he said, 'Come again Tuesday!'

'But it's Tuesday today,' objected the woman.

The shoemaker let his spectacles fall back on his nose.

'Come again Wednesday!' he snapped and went on with his work.

'Oh, you're just the same old lazy sour-puss that you always were!' said the woman, and left him to it.

In the afternoon a little boy started playing in the

street outside the house. He came to the door and asked the shoemaker to button his jacket because his fingers were too cold to manage the buttonhole.

'Come again Thursday!' said the shoemaker in his snappy voice.

'But I'm cold today, mister!' said the little boy.

'Come again Friday!' said the shoemaker.

'You're just a grumpy old toad, so you are!' said the little boy, and went away.

'Good riddance!' said the shoemaker, and he didn't even turn round, but went on with his work, mending and patching till it was too dark to work any more. Then he ate up the rest of the loaf and climbed into bed. But in his sleep he dreamed that the doll came over to him and this is what she said:

'I can button, mend a hose,
I can wipe a runny nose,
If *you* won't, *I* will!'

'You're a proper fusspot, aren't you?' said the shoemaker when he woke in the morning and remembered his dream. 'I'd better get those shoes finished for Mrs Butt. Then when I take them along to her I can take the ring for the little girl as well.'

So he sat down at his bench and finished mending Mrs Butt's shoes.

Meanwhile the little boy had started playing outside the window again; the shoemaker called him in.

'Come here, boy, let me button your coat for you,' he said. 'Would you like me to wipe that nose of yours too? You can tell me if it hurts.'

' 'Course it doesn't hurt,' said the little boy, blowing into the hankie like a trumpet and waving his fingers in the air; they were quite stiff and blue with cold. 'Not so cross today, are you?' he said, and then he added: 'I'd like to help *you* now. Got any messages for me to take?'

'Well yes, I have, as a matter of fact,' said the shoemaker. 'You can take these shoes to Mrs Butt at the corner, and while you're at it you can take this ring and give it to the little girl at Crag House; she lost it here a long time ago.'

'All right!' said the little boy and ran off with the things.

It wasn't long before he was back with a message from Mrs Butt. 'Mrs Butt told me to tell you that if you want your Sunday suit cleaned and pressed she'd be glad to do it for you. And that girl at Crag House told me to thank you and ask if you'd like to go to her birthday party tomorrow—she's asked me too, wasn't that nice of her?'

The shoemaker was staring in front of him, thinking hard. 'Very nice of her, I'm sure. But, as for me, I've been on my own for so long now I wouldn't know how to behave with other folks at a party. No, I'd better not go.'

But when the little boy had gone away and the shoemaker had got into bed he dreamed again that the doll came over to speak to him:

'I always smile when folks are kind,
Not turn my back and act so blind,
If *you* won't, *I* will!'

Next morning the shoemaker remembered and said to himself, 'I shall have to go, then.' And he has never regretted it. For one thing, he wore his Sunday suit, all neatly cleaned and pressed by Mrs Butt, and, for another, he had three different kinds of cake to eat, and, most important of all, he found out that it is good for people to get together now and then and not always to be moping on their own.

Ever since that day the shoemaker's cottage has been as clean as a new pin, and the shoemaker himself whistles and sings as he goes about his housework. He makes his bed and scrubs the floor, he buttons boys' coats and wipes their noses and he mends the shoes in double-quick time.

Every now and again, when there's something he *doesn't* want to do, he takes a quick look at his doll on the chest of drawers, and he always ends up by doing whatever it is he has to do. For if *he* won't, *she* will.

Mrs Pepperpot is taken for a Witch

Mrs Pepperpot lives in a valley in Norway, and in summertime in that part of the world the nights hardly get dark at all. On Midsummer's Eve, in fact, the sun never quite goes down, so everybody, young and old, stays up all night to dance and sing and let off fireworks round a big bonfire. And because there's magic abroad on Midsummer's Eve they sometimes see witches riding on broomsticks through the sky—or they think they do, anyway.

Now the only two people in that valley who never used to go to the bonfire party were Mr and Mrs Pepperpot. Not that Mrs Pepperpot didn't want to go, but Midsummer's Eve happened to be Mr Pepperpot's birthday as well, and on that day it was he who decided what they did. He never liked mixing with a crowd on account of that shrinking habit of Mrs Pepperpot; he was always afraid that she would suddenly turn the size of a pepperpot and disappear, leaving him standing there looking a proper fool.

But this year Mrs Pepperpot *did* go to the party, and this is how it happened.

It started the night before Midsummer's Eve. Mrs Pepperpot had been to the store and was walking slowly home with her basket on her arm. She was wondering how she could persuade her husband to go to the bonfire when suddenly she had an idea.

'I could ask him if there was something he really wanted for his birthday, and then I could say I would give it to him if he promised to take me to the bonfire party.'

As soon as she got inside the door she jumped on her husband's knee and gave him a smacking kiss on the tip of his nose.

'Dear, good hubby,' she said, 'have you got a very special wish for your birthday tomorrow?'

Her husband was quite surprised. 'Have you had sunstroke or something? How could you buy anything? Why, money runs through your fingers like water.'

'Sometimes it does, and sometimes it doesn't,' said Mrs Pepperpot, looking sly; 'there are such things as hens, and hens lay eggs and eggs can be sold. Just now I have quite a tidy sum put by, so just you tell me what you would like and the present will be laid out here on the table as sure as my name's Pepperpot.'

'Well,' he said, 'if you think you have enough money to buy that handsome pipe with the silver band that's lying in the store window, I'll promise you something in return.'

'Done!' cried Mrs Pepperpot at once, 'and the thing I want you to promise me is to take me to the bonfire party on Windy Ridge tomorrow night!'

So Mr Pepperpot had to agree and the next day Mrs Pepperpot filled her pockets with all the sixpennies, pennies and threepenny bits she had earned from the eggs and set off to the store.

'I want to buy the pipe with the silver band,' said Mrs Pepperpot, when it came to her turn to be served.

But the grocer shook his head. 'Sorry, Mrs Pepperpot,'

he said, 'but I'm afraid I sold that pipe to Peter Poulsen yesterday.'

'Oh dear,' said Mrs Pepperpot, 'I'll have to go and see if he'll let me buy it off him,' and she hurried out of the door, letting the door-bell jingle loudly as she went.

She took the shortest way to Peter Poulsen's house, but when she got there only his wife was at home.

'I was wondering if your husband would sell me that pipe he bought in the store yesterday?' said Mrs Pepperpot. 'I'd pay him well for it,' she added, and patted her pocketful of coins.

'That pipe is no longer in the house,' said Mrs Poulsen, who had a sour look on her face. 'I wasn't going to have tobacco smoke in my curtains, no *thank* you! I gave it to some boys who were having a sale; they said they were collecting money for fireworks for tonight's bonfire, or some such nonsense.'

Mrs Pepperpot's heart sank; did Mrs Poulsen know where the sale was being held?

'Up on Windy Ridge, near the bonfire, the boys said,' answered Mrs Poulsen, and Mrs Pepperpot lost no time in making her way up to Windy Ridge.

But it was a tidy walk uphill and when she got to the top she found the boys had sold everything. They were busy tidying up the bits of paper and string and cardboard boxes and carrying them over to the bonfire.

Mrs Pepperpot was so out of breath her tongue was hanging out, but she managed to stammer, 'Who got the pipe?'

'What pipe?' asked one of the boys.

'The one with the silver band that Mrs Poulsen gave you.'

'Oh that,' said the boy; 'my brother bought it. But then he tried to smoke it and it made him sick. So he got fed up with it and tied it to a long pole and stuck it at the top of the bonfire. There it is—look!'

Mrs Pepperpot looked, and there it was, right enough, tied to a pole at the very top of the huge bonfire!

'Couldn't you take it down again?' she asked the boy.

'Are you crazy?' said the boy. 'Expect us to upset the bonfire when we've got everything piled up just nicely? Not likely! Besides, we're going to have some fun with that pipe; you wait and see! But I can't stand talking now, I must go and get a can of petrol to start it off.' And he ran off with the other boys.

'Oh dear, oh dear, oh dear!' wailed Mrs Pepperpot,

to herself. 'I see there's nothing for it but to climb that bonfire and get it down myself.' But she looked with dismay at the mountain of old mattresses, broken chairs, table-legs, barrows, drawers, old clothes and hats, car-tyres and empty cartons.

'First I shall have to find a stick to poke the pipe off the pole when I do get up aloft,' she thought.

Just at that moment she turned small, but for once Mrs Pepperpot was really pleased. 'Hooray!' she shouted in her shrill little voice. 'It won't take long for a little thing like me to get that pipe down now, and I don't even need to upset the bonfire!'

Quick as a mouse, she darted into the big pile and started climbing up from the inside. But it was not as easy as she had thought; climbing over a mattress she got her heel stuck in a spring and it took her quite a while to free herself. Then she had difficulty in climbing a slippery chair-leg; she kept sliding back. But at last she managed it, only to find herself entangled in the lining of a coat. She groped about in this for some time before she found her way out of the sleeve.

By now people had started gathering round the bonfire.

'All right, let them have a good look,' she thought. 'Luckily I'm too small for them to see me up here. And nothing's going to stop me from getting to the top now!'

Just then she lost her grip and fell into a deep drawer. There she lay, puffing and blowing, till she managed to catch hold of a bonnet string which was hanging over the edge of the drawer.

'Not much further to go, thank goodness!' she told herself, but when she looked down she almost fainted; it was fearfully far to the ground, and now there were crowds of people standing round, waiting for the bonfire to be lit.

'No time to lose!' thought Mrs Pepperpot, and heaved herself on to the last obstacle. This was easy, because it was an old concertina, so she could walk up it like a staircase.

Now she was at the foot of the pole and at the top was the pipe, securely tied!

'However am I going to get up there?' she wondered, but then she noticed the rim of an empty tar-barrel right next to her. So she smeared a little tar on her hands to give them a better grip, and then she started to climb the pole. But the pole and the whole bonfire seemed to be heeling a little over to one side, and when she looked down she nearly fell off with fright: *the boys had lit the bonfire!*

Little flames were licking up round the mattresses and the broken furniture.

Then people started cheering and the children chanted: 'Wait till it gets to the pipe at the top! Wait till it gets to the pipe at the top!'

'Catch me waiting!' muttered Mrs Pepperpot. 'I've got to get there *first*!' and she climbed on up till her hands gripped the stem of the pipe. Down below she could hear the children shouting:

'Watch the flames when they reach the pole! There's a rocket tied to the pipe!'

'Oh, good gracious!' cried Mrs Pepperpot, clinging on for dear life. BANG! Up into the cold night sky shot the rocket, the pole, the pipe *and* Mrs Pepperpot!

Round the bonfire everyone suddenly stopped shouting. A thin woman in a shawl whispered to her neighbour:

'I thought I saw someone sitting on that stick!'

Her neighbour, who was even thinner and wore two shawls, whispered back, 'It could have been a witch!' and they both shuddered. But from behind them came a man's voice:

'Oh, it couldn't be her, could it?' It was Mr Pepperpot who had just left off working and had taken a ride up to the mountain to have a look at the bonfire. Now he swung himself on his bicycle again and raced home as fast as he could go, muttering all the way, 'Let her be at home; oh, please let her be at home!' When he reached the house and opened the door his hand was shaking.

There stood Mrs Pepperpot, quite her normal size and with no sign of a broomstick. She was decorating his birthday cake and on the table, neatly laid on a little cloth, was the precious pipe with its silver band.

'Many Happy Returns of the Day!' said Mrs Pepperpot. 'Come and have your meal now. Then you can put

on a clean shirt and take your wife to dance all night at the bonfire party!'

'Anything you say!' said Mr Pepperpot; he was so relieved she hadn't gone off with the witches of Midsummer's Eve.

The Little Mouse who was Very Clever

THERE WAS once a little mouse called Squeak, who sat behind the door in his mousehole, waiting for his mother to come home from the larder with some food.

Suddenly there was a knock at the door.

'Who is that?' asked little Squeak.

'Peep, peep, let me in, it's your mother,' said a voice outside, but it didn't sound a mousy sort of voice.

'Why are you knocking at our door?'

'I forgot to take the key,' said the voice.

'We don't use a key for this door,' said the little mouse.

'It's bolted on the inside and I'm not opening it for *you*!'

Whoever it was went away and Squeak waited for some time before there came another knock.

'Who is that?' asked Squeak.

'It's Peter,' said a voice, but it didn't sound like Peter, the little boy who lived in the house.

'Why are you knocking at our door?'

'Because you've been using my shawl for your bed,' said the voice.

'If you're a little boy, you won't want a shawl,' said Squeak. 'I'm not opening the door for you!'

After he had waited some time there was another knock.

'Who is that?' he asked.

'Peter's mother,' came the reply; 'let me in.'

'Why are you knocking at our door?'

'Because I think you must have hidden my braces down your hole,' said the voice, which sounded rather purry for a lady.

'If you are Peter's mother,' said little Squeak, 'I'm sure you don't need braces. I'm not opening the door for *you*!'

Again he had to wait a long time before the next knock.

'Who is that?' said Squeak.

'This is Peter's father,' said a voice that was very croaky. 'Let me in at once!'

'Why are you knocking at our door?' asked the little mouse.

'My tail went in the honey-pot and I want you to clean it.'

'If you are Peter's father,' said Squeak, 'why have you got a tail? I'm not opening the door for *you*!'

After that there was a long, long silence, and then at last there was a tiny little knock.

'Who is that?' asked Squeak.

'It's your mother, darling.'

But the little mouse wanted to make quite sure:

'Why are you knocking at our door?'

'Because I want my clever Squeak to unbolt it as he always does,' said the voice. Then he knew it was his mother, and the little mouse, who was too clever to be tricked by a cat with many voices, unbolted the door and let his mother in.

And because he'd been so clever his mother gave him an extra large lump of cheese for his supper.

Mrs Pepperpot's Birthday

IT WAS Mrs Pepperpot's birthday, so she had asked her neighbours in to coffee at three o'clock. All day she had been scrubbing and polishing, and now it was ten minutes to three and she was putting the final touches to the strawberry layer cake on the kitchen table. As she stood balancing the last strawberry on a spoon, she suddenly felt herself shrinking, not slowly as she sometimes did, but so fast that she didn't even have time to put the strawberry on a plate. It rolled on to the floor and Mrs Pepperpot tumbled after it. But she quickly picked herself up and jumped into the cat's basket. Puss was a bit surprised, but allowed her to snuggle down with the kittens. In her black-and-white-striped skirt and white blouse, she hoped the guests would take her for one of the cat-family, until the magic wore off and she could be her real size again. For you may remember that Mrs Pepperpot never liked anyone to see her when she was tiny.

There was a knock at the door, and, when it wasn't

answered, Sarah from South Farm walked into the little front hall, carrying a huge bunch of lilac.

'Many Happy Returns of the Day!' said Sarah. There was no reply, so she peered into the kitchen, thinking Mrs Pepperpot might be in there, though, naturally, she didn't look in the cat-basket. Somehow she managed to knock over the flower-vase on the hall table, and the water spilled on the tablecloth and on to the floor.

'Oh dear, oh dear!' thought Sarah. 'I shall have to mop that up before anybody notices.'

But at that moment there was another knock at the

door. So Sarah ran into the kitchen and hid in a cupboard.

In came Norah from North Farm, and she was carrying a very nice tablecloth.

'Many Happy Returns!' she said, but, as she got no answer, she looked round for Mrs Pepperpot, and her parcel swept the vase off the table on to the floor.

'That's bad!' thought Norah. 'I must put it back before anybody comes.'

But before she could do it there was another knock on the door and Norah hurried into the bedroom and crept under the bed.

Esther from East Farm came in, carrying a handsome glass bowl for Mrs Pepperpot. When she had said 'Many Happy Returns!' and no one answered, she walked

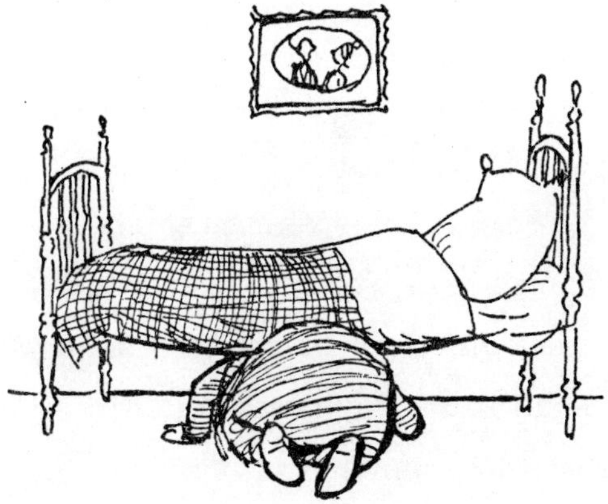

straight into the living-room. Carrying the bowl in front of her, she didn't notice the vase on the floor and put her foot straight on it. There was a nasty crunch and there it lay, in smithereens!

'Goodness gracious, what have I done?' thought Esther. 'Perhaps if I hide behind this curtain no one will know who did it!' So she quickly wrapped herself in one of the curtains.

At that moment the clock struck three, and the magic wore off; there was Mrs Pepperpot as large as life, walking through the kitchen. 'Coo-ee!' she called. 'You can all come out now!'

So Sarah stepped out of the cupboard, Norah crawled from under the bed, while Esther unwrapped herself from the curtain in the living-room.

At first they looked a bit sheepish, but then they said 'Many Happy Returns!' all over again and they had a good laugh, while Mrs Pepperpot swept up the broken vase, threw away the dead flowers and put the wet tablecloth in the wash-tub.

Then she thanked them for their fine presents; the table was spread with Norah's tablecloth, Esther's glass bowl was filled with fresh water, and the huge bunch of lilac that Sarah had brought was put into it.

After that Mrs Pepperpot brought in the coffee and

cakes and they all sat down to enjoy themselves. But on the strawberry layer cake there was one strawberry missing.

'You see,' said Mrs Pepperpot, when they asked her what had happened to it, 'my *first* visitor this afternoon was the little old woman who shrinks, and she was so tiny today that one strawberry was all she could manage to eat. So I gave her that and a thimble of milk to wash it down.'

'Didn't you ask her to stay, so that we could see her?' asked Sarah, for they were all very curious about the little old woman who shrank, and nobody thereabouts had ever seen her.

'She was sorry, she said, but she was in a tearing hurry; she had some business with a mouse, her night watchman or something. But she told me to tell you she did enjoy our little game of hide-and-seek!'

The Dancing Bees

YOU HAVE probably been told that bees are very busy, hardworking creatures, collecting honey from the flowers from morning till night all through the summer to store it up for food in winter.

But now you shall hear about a she-bee who spent her time in quite a different way; she did nothing but dance. And what gave her this curious idea? Well, wait till I tell you.

One evening in June this she-bee was on her way home to the hive from the meadows, but she hadn't found any honey that day. So when she saw a beautiful flower right below her she swooped down and settled on it. But the flower was swinging round because it was fixed to a hat, and the hat was on the head of a girl, and the girl was dancing with her young man to the band in People's Park.

At first the little she-bee was disappointed to find no honey in the flower, but soon she forgot all about it; it

was such a delicious feeling to sway up and down in time to the music.

'It's like hearing a thousand bumble-bees humming over a field of clover,' she murmured happily as she swayed round and round.

'Yes, isn't it?' said a voice quite close to her. And there, on the boy's hat, sat another bee!

'I shouldn't talk to strangers, I know,' said the little she-bee, 'but this music is making me so giddy I don't really know what I'm doing.'

'Nothing wrong in talking, surely?' said the other bee, who was, of course, a he-bee. 'Allow me to say that you dance superbly, and it's not so easy to hang on to a flower that is swinging round and round. I know what I'm talking about; there were two young lady bees here earlier this summer and I tried to dance with them, but they both fell off after just a few turns. I always hold on to the young man's hat-brim; in any case, this is my second season here, so I've had plenty of practice. Ah, the music is stopping; that means it's time for refreshments. Just stay where you are.'

The girl and the young man moved over to the refreshment tent and the bees went with them on their hats.

'Do you live far from here?' asked the he-bee.

'It's quite a long flight,' said the she-bee, 'but I simply daren't let anyone see me home, as we have such a very strict doorkeeper.'

'I quite understand,' he replied, 'but perhaps you will permit me to fetch you a little drink of fruit-juice?'

He flew down on to the table and a moment later brought back a drop of fruit-juice on one of his wings. 'Excuse my wing, but it is the only way I can manage it.'

'Very nice of you to bother; thank you very much,' said the little she-bee. 'Aren't you having any yourself?'

'Not for me, thanks, I'm driving—at least, it's not exactly *me* driving, but I daren't take any risks, all the same. I shall have to get back to my own hat now, I see they're starting the show.'

The little she-bee would have liked to ask what a 'show' was, but she felt shy, so she just rubbed her wings with her feet.

'Tonight there's a fellow with a guitar—forgotten his name, but he's very famous,' the he-bee told her. 'One young lady bee told me she once sat on his guitar while he played "Rocking round the Clock", and she'll never forget it as long as she lives, she said.'

The little she-bee listened while the man on the platform sang and played his guitar, and very funny he looked. First he sang quite quietly, but suddenly he went into shrieks and sobs and then he fell right down on his knees and shuffled off the platform backwards.

'What happened? Did a bee sting him?' asked the she-bee.

'No, no, that was the high spot,' answered her new friend.

'The high spot? Oh yes, I've heard that high spots can sting very badly—the poor man!' And the little she-bee felt quite sorry for the man. But then the music began once more. 'Isn't it wonderful!' she cried, and clapped her front pair of feet.

They sailed out on the dance-floor again, she on her flower and he on his hat-brim.

'I'm afraid that's the last dance tonight,' he said. 'I can see they're beginning to put out the lights.'

'How sad! I shall have to hurry home now,' said the little she-bee, 'but thank you so much for a lovely evening.'

'You're welcome! Perhaps we could meet another time?'

'That would be very nice,' she answered.

When she got back to the hive the doorkeeper would not let her in at first because she had no honey with her. But in the end he relented.

Next evening she went dancing again. But this time

she was careful to hide a little honey in a tree-stump close to the hive, so that she could pick it up on her way home after the dance.

The he-bee on his hat-brim was very pleased to see her. 'I have been thinking about you all day,' he said.

'Very kind of you, I'm sure,' she said, looking very demure.

Like the evening before, there was music, there was dancing, the he-bee brought her fruit-juice, and then there was the show. Afterwards he persuaded her to take a little ride in the young man's car, but when the he-bee asked if he might sit on *her* hat the little she-bee said firmly, 'No.'

Later, when she got back to the hive, she had no difficulty in getting past the doorkeeper, as she had remembered her store of honey in the tree-stump.

And so it went on every evening all through the summer, and no one in the hive knew anything about it. But one day, while the she-bee was flying round looking for honey, she forgot herself; instead of her ordinary buzzing song she started to sing 'Waltzing Matilda'.

'Whatever are you buzzing?' asked the bee who was flying nearest to her.

The little she-bee got quite confused. 'It's—it's only a little waltz tune I heard,' she stammered. Then, of course, she had to explain *where* she had heard it. But this was just as well, for she could not have kept the secret to herself much longer.

As the day went on other bees kept flying up to her wanting her to tell them about the dancing, the music and the show, and about her dancing partner on the hat-brim.

'Can't you take us along with you tonight?' they all pleaded.

'Not tonight,' she said, 'but perhaps tomorrow, if my partner gives his permission.'

That evening was as delightful as all the rest, but the young man didn't have his car with him, so he and the girl and the bees all went for a walk in the wood instead.

'It is really just as pleasant, don't you think, to go for a walk on such a lovely evening?' said the he-bee. 'And if I'm not mistaken we're heading for that little bank with the bluebells on it.' He was right; the young man and the girl sat down on the flowery bank, and so did the two bees.

The young man spoke softly to the girl, and she bent her head so far forward that the bee had to hold on tight not to fall off the flower.

'Why does she bend her head like that?' she asked.

'He is proposing to her,' said the he-bee. 'You had

better let me come over and hold you so you don't fall off.' And he took off from the hat-brim and made an elegant landing on the flower. Then he put his wing protectingly round the little she-bee. This time she did not protest.

'What does "propose" mean?' she asked, though deep inside she had a feeling she knew what it meant already.

'He is asking if she will be his wife and stay with him for ever.'

'Oh, how wonderful!' cried the little she-bee before she could stop herself.

'Do you really think so? Then I shall propose to you this very minute,' said the he-bee, 'even though this isn't the usual way for bees to behave, I'm sure. But it's difficult, you will agree, not to be carried away in these beautiful surroundings and hearing so much love-talk!'

'Oh yes!' sighed the little she-bee, and hung her head bashfully just like the young girl.

The next day there was a terrific hullabaloo in the hive. The bees who knew about the dancing had told a lot more bees, and now it had got all round the hive. There they were, a great black swarm of them, thronging round the entrance, all demanding to go to People's Park like the little she-bee.

'Show us the way!' they kept crying. 'Show us the way and we'll follow you!'

The little she-bee hesitated at first, but then she said: 'All right, I will. You can all come with me.' Secretly she was longing for the music and for her partner in the park.

So the whole swarm rose in the air and flew off after the she-bee. But this was in the middle of the day and there was not a soul to be seen in People's Park when they got there. No sign of the flower on the hat, or, for that matter, of the girl and the young man and the he-bee. The she-bee was lost and she knew it, but she couldn't stop now.

On, on she flew, and the swarm after her, over fields and meadows, over roads and hedges, until quite suddenly the little she-bee caught sight of something hanging on the branch of an apple tree.

It was the hat with the flower on it! She was saved!

'Come on, all of you!' she buzzed as loudly as she could. She flew to the flower and clung there. And all the other bees clung to her, till they looked like a huge black cluster of grapes shining in the sunshine.

Someone came into the orchard; it was the girl. When she saw what was happening to her hat she gave a shriek of alarm. She shouted out to someone inside the house, and out came the young man with a great big net. He put it carefully over the swarm of bees and carried it over to an empty hive. There he shook the net so that they all tumbled in, and then he put the lid on firmly.

As luck would have it, the he-bee was still perched on the young man's hat-brim, so he was able to slip into the hive with the rest of them.

After they had time to settle down in their new home the bees made the little she-bee their queen. But, from what I've heard, she was not a bit kind to the he-bee when he became her husband. And if he or any of the other bees ever dared to dream about going dancing in People's Park they soon discovered that it was the queen who called the tune from now on; their dancing days were over for good.

How the King Learned to Eat Porridge

THERE WAS once a king who was wise and good and mighty and rich, but he had one fault. Not a very big fault, mind you, but annoying enough. And do you know what it was?

He would not eat porridge.

Now this wouldn't have mattered so much if he had kept it to himself. After all, a king has so many other things to eat. But he was an honest king, so he could not lie, and he told both the government and the people that he did not like porridge.

'I detest porridge!' he declared. 'It tastes of glue and tufts of wool. Ugh!'

And when the people of his realm heard that they wouldn't eat porridge either. They wanted to be like the king—especially the children, who thought it was wonderful not to eat porridge, and whooped with delight. On the national flag-day they walked in the procession carrying big banners saying 'Long Live the King! Down with Porridge!'

But far up in the mountains there lived a peasant with his daughter, and they had only one tiny field of their own. On this field they grew oats, and their whole livelihood depended on it. So when everyone stopped buying oats they made less and less money.

'This can't go on!' said the peasant's daughter one day. 'People not eating porridge like this. I shall have to go to the palace and give that stupid king a piece of my mind!'

'Take care, my child, you might make the king angry,' said her father.

'He'd better take care himself,' she answered, 'or *I* might get angry.' And she slung a bag of oatmeal over her shoulder and set off for the palace.

In the palace garden she met a man, but the country girl did not know he was really the king.

'Where are you off to?' asked the man.

'I'm going to the palace to teach the king to eat porridge,' she answered.

This made the man laugh. 'If you can do that,' he said, 'you're a very clever girl!' Then he went into the royal kitchen and told the royal cook that he could take a day off, as a country girl had come to town to teach him, the king, to eat porridge.

Next day, when the king was at breakfast, the

peasant's daughter brought in a big steaming bowl of porridge. She was a little taken aback when she saw who the man was she had spoken to in the garden. But the king smiled at her and said:

'Come along now, you must teach me to eat this porridge of yours.'

'Oh no,' she said, 'not after making such a fool of

myself, I couldn't. Anyway, I don't suppose you even know which hand to hold the spoon in?'

'I think I do,' said the king, and picked up the spoon in his right hand.

'Just as I thought!' said the girl. 'Never in all my life have I seen anyone eat porridge with the right hand!'

'All right,' said the king, 'I'll try with my left hand.'

'That's better,' said the girl, 'but I've never seen anyone with a bowl of porridge on the table while they sat on a chair to eat it. Get up on the table and put the bowl on the chair in the proper manner!'

The king was beginning to enjoy himself. First he got

up on the table and then he tried to set the bowl on the chair. But this was not so easy; he nearly lost his balance several times before he managed it.

'There, now you can start eating,' said the girl.

The king held the spoon in his left hand and bent down to the bowl. It was awkward, but he succeeded at last in getting a spoonful up to his mouth and swallowing it.

'Just a minute,' said the girl, 'you have to hold your left ear with your right hand while you're eating.'

'I expect I can manage that too,' said the king, and balanced another spoonful up to his mouth.

'That's only two spoonfuls,' she said. 'Wait till you get to the bottom of the bowl; that's when it gets really difficult.'

'Don't worry, I'll do it!' said the king, and, do you know, he didn't give in till he had scraped the bowl clean!

'There you are!' he shouted proudly.

'There you are yourself!' said the girl. 'Now I have taught the king to eat porridge!'

At first the king was a little put out that she had tricked him in this way. But then he had to laugh.

'You're a very cunning little girl,' he said. 'I almost think I'll marry you—that is, if you're willing?'

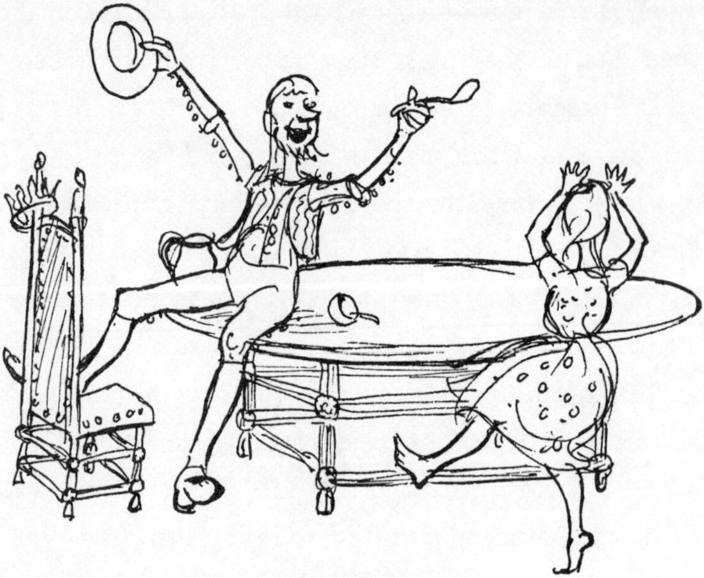

'I might as well,' said the girl.

* * * * *

So they were married, and at the wedding a huge pot of hot, steaming porridge was set up in the middle of the market place, and the king commanded his people, including the whole court and all his ministers, to come and learn how to eat porridge.

The queen stood on a high tribune to teach them, and they all laughed and enjoyed themselves like anything. But when they had had their lesson the queen said:

'Now I know you can all eat porridge; so from this day on you may sit on your chairs and put your porridge bowls on the table and eat it the way you do any other food.'

But many people, especially the children, preferred the way the queen had taught them and went on doing it—secretly.

Mrs Pepperpot Turns Fortune-Teller

EVERY MORNING when Mr Pepperpot goes off to work Mrs Pepperpot stands at the window and watches him till he disappears round the bend to the main road. Then

she settles down in the chair by the kitchen table, picks up her empty coffee cup and starts reading her fortune in it.

Now you probably didn't know that Mrs Pepperpot could read fortunes in a cup. Well, she can; she can tell from the way the coffee grounds lie what road she will take that day and whether she will meet joy or sorrow before nightfall. Sometimes she sees the shape of a heart in the cup and that means she will have a new sweetheart. But that makes Mrs Pepperpot laugh, for to her it means she will probably get a new pet to look after—perhaps a poor little bird with a broken wing or a stray kitten on her doorstep, getting tamer and tamer as it laps up the food and milk she gives it.

But if the grounds form a cross she knows she must watch her step, for that means she will break something; it could be when she is washing up or when she is scrubbing the floor. If she sees a clear drop of coffee running down the side of the cup that means she will hurt herself in some way and will need not only a bandage but maybe a doctor as well. And so it goes on; there are many more signs that she can read, but she only does it for herself, never for other people, even if they ask her. It's just an amusement, she says, something to while away the time when she is at home alone all day.

Well, this day—it was a Friday too—Mrs Pepperpot had planned to give the house a good clean out and then she was going to bake a cake for Mr Pepperpot. Apart from that she was just going to take it easy for a change. So, when she had watched her husband turn the corner, she picked up their two coffee cups and was just about to put them in the sink. But then she stopped herself.

'There, what am I doing? I nearly forgot to have a look at my fortune for today!' So she took one of the cups back to the table and sat down. 'Let's see, now,' she said and turned the cup round and round in her hand. 'Oh dear, oh dear!' she exclaimed, 'what's this I see? A big cross? I shall have to mind how I go today and no mistake!'

At that very moment she shrank, and in no time at all she was no bigger than the coffee cup and both she and the cup fell off the chair on to the floor.

'That was a bit of a come-down!' she said, and felt both her arms and her legs to see if there were any bones broken. But when she found she was still all in one piece she lay still for a moment, not daring to look at the cup. For it was one of her best ones, and she was sure it must have been broken by the fall.

At last she said to herself, 'I suppose I shall have to have a look.' And when she did she found to her

great surprise that the cup was not even cracked or chipped.

But she was still worried. 'If that isn't it there'll be something else for me to break today,' she said miserably as she squatted down to look into the cup, for it was lying on its side.

'Oh me, oh my!' she cried. 'If this isn't my unlucky day!' She had caught sight of a large clear drop on the side of the cup. 'This means tears, but I wonder what will make me cry?'

Suddenly there was a loud BANG! inside the kitchen cupboard. Mrs Pepperpot nearly jumped out of her skin with fright.

'There! Now isn't that just like Mr P., setting a mouse-trap in the cupboard, although he knows it's not necessary now that I have a mouse for a night watchman. It's only now and again that a baby mouse gets into the cupboard by mistake—before he's learned the mouse rules. It's not as if they *mean* to do any damage, so it's silly to take any notice. I wonder if I dare open the door a little to see what's happened? I suppose I'd better; the little thing might just have caught its tail and I could free it. But, of course, it might be worse than that; the cup said tears, and tears it will be, no doubt!'

So Mrs Pepperpot went over to the cupboard and pulled gently at the door. But she closed her eyes to keep back the tears which were ready to come at any moment. When she had the door opened enough to look in she opened first one eye, then the other, and then she flopped down on the floor, clapping her hands on her knees, and burst out laughing.

Right enough, the trap had snapped, but there was nothing in it. Instead two baby mice were happily playing just beside it with two empty cotton-reels. Mrs Pepperpot thought it was the funniest sight she'd ever seen.

'Hullo, Mrs Pepperpot!' squealed one of the baby mice. 'Have you shrunk again?'

'We hoped you would!' said the other one, ' 'cos my brother and I had never seen you small before, and

Granny said we could come in here and have a peep—just in case you shrunk. We weren't being naughty—just playing cars—and then we bumped into that nasty thing which went snap over there.'

'Will you play with us?' asked the first little mouse. 'You sit in the car and we'll pull you along.'

And when Mrs Pepperpot looked closer she saw that the baby mice had fixed a matchbox over the cotton-reels and the whole contraption really moved.

'Let's go!' shouted Mrs Pepperpot, and jumped into the box.

So they played at cars, taking turns to sit in the matchbox, and Mrs Pepperpot laughed while the baby mice squealed with delight, till, all of a sudden, they heard a scratching sound above them.

'That's enough, children!' called granny mouse,

whose head had appeared in a hole in the back wall. 'The cat's on top of the cupboard and the door is open!'

Before you could say 'knife' the two baby mice had disappeared through the hole, squeaking 'Thanks for the game!' as they went.

'Thank you!' said Mrs Pepperpot, and stepped out of the cupboard to see what that cat was up to.

There she was, standing on top of the cupboard waving her tail expectantly when Mrs Pepperpot came out. But Mrs Pepperpot was not standing any nonsense; she shouted at the cat: 'What are you doing up there? You get down at once or I'll teach you a lesson as soon as I grow again! Maybe it's you who are going to break something for me today? Yes, I can feel it in my bones. I know if I have another look in that cup there'll be more calamity there for me.'

By now she was just as worked up as she had been before her little game with the mice. But she couldn't resist having another look in the cup. 'Goodness gracious!' she cried. 'It's just as I thought, doctor and bandages, ambulances and everything! As if I hadn't trouble enough already! Down you get, cat, and make it quick!'

'All right! Keep your hair on,' said the cat. 'I was only doing my duty when I heard a suspicious noise in the cupboard. I'm coming down now.'

'Mind how you go! Be careful! I don't want anything broken. I'll stand here below and direct you,' said Mrs Pepperpot.

'Anybody would think I'd never jumped off a cupboard before, and I'm not in the habit of breaking things,' answered the cat, as he made his way gingerly past a big china bowl. But just on the edge of the cupboard lay a large pair of scissors, and neither the cat nor Mrs Pepperpot had seen them.

Mrs Pepperpot was busy with her warnings: 'Mind that bowl!' she shouted, standing right beneath those scissors.

The cat was being as careful as she could, but her tail brushed against the scissors, sending them flying, point downwards, to the floor. There they stood quivering!

Mrs Pepperpot had just managed to jump out of the way, but now she was too frightened to move. 'So that was it!' she stammered at last. She felt herself all over again, for this time she was *sure* she must be hurt. But she couldn't find as much as a scratch!

A moment later she was her normal size. So she pulled the scissors out of the floor and lifted the cat down out of harm's way. Then she set to work cleaning the house and just had time to bake her cake before she heard her husband at the door.

But what a state he was in! The tears were pouring out of his eyes because of the bitter wind outside, and anyway he had a bad cold. One hand he was holding behind his back: he had fallen off his bicycle, had broken his cycle lamp and cut his hand on the glass!

As she hurriedly searched for something to tie round his hand, Mrs Pepperpot thought how odd it was that it was Mr Pepperpot who had tears in his eyes; it was Mr Pepperpot that had broken something, and had hurt himself so that he had to have a bandage on. Very odd indeed!

But if you think this cured Mrs Pepperpot of reading her fortune in a coffee cup you are very much mistaken. The only thing is, she *does* take more care not to pick up the wrong cup and read her husband's fortune instead of her own.

The Fairy-Tale Boy

ONCE UPON A TIME there was a little boy who said to his mother, 'I want to go out into the world and kill a dragon, and then I'll bring you back all the gold.'

His mother answered: 'But what about the princess? Won't you set her free as well, pet?'

'I suppose so,' said George, for that was his name, 'as long as I don't have to marry her; 'cos you know I don't like girls.'

'Very well, dear; good luck!' said his mother.

'Oh, but you mustn't just say "good luck!" You have to give me food and drink for the journey. I'm going to sit down by the side of the road and start eating, and then an old woman will come or a dwarf, or something like that, and they'll be hungry, and I'll give them all my food, 'cos then they'll help me, you know, to find the way to the dragon and all that.'

'All right, pet, you shall have some food for the journey,' said his mother, and she put three sandwiches in a tin and put them in a little knapsack with a bottle of milk.

So George went out into the world to kill the dragon. And when he had walked a little he came to a road crossing and there he sat down and opened his knapsack and took out a sandwich.

'I 'spect an old woman will come along in a minute, and she'll ask me for food. Then afterwards she's sure to show me the way to the dragon,' he said to himself.

No sooner had he thought this than an old woman

did come round the corner, walking slowly towards him. When she reached the place where he was sitting she stopped and fixed her eyes on George's sandwich.

'Good afternoon,' said George, and held out his hand with the sandwich in it.

'Good afternoon, my boy,' said the woman; 'you shouldn't play with your food like that.'

'I'm *not* playing with my food,' said George indignantly. 'I'm giving it to you. Aren't you hungry?'

'Of course not,' said the woman. 'I have my lunch before I go out, and so should you, young fellow, and not drag it about with you, leaving dirty bits of paper behind and egg-shells and I don't know what. Ugh!' And with that she walked off and left George holding his sandwich.

George sat staring after her for a bit.

'Oh well,' he said, 'I suppose there'll be others coming along. She wasn't the right kind of fairy-tale woman, anyway. I'd better eat this sandwich myself while I'm waiting.'

While he was munching the bread he heard a scuffling noise behind the hedge. It was a squirrel.

'Hullo, squirrel! Would you like something to eat?' said George, and threw the second sandwich into the hedge. But the squirrel took fright and bounded away towards a wood.

'Perhaps it wants me to follow it,' thought George. So he picked up his knapsack and walked after the squirrel to the wood. The squirrel, meanwhile, stayed quite still, as if it were really waiting for him, and George was now quite certain that it was going to show him the way to the dragon. When he got quite close the squirrel started leaping from branch to branch and George began to run, stumbling over sticks and stumps, further and further into the wood, until at last they came to a little stream. Here the squirrel jumped lightly from a tree on one side of the stream to another tree on the other side. But George stopped; the stream was too deep for him to wade across, and he was afraid he might drown. So he very sensibly stayed where he was.

Instead he sat down by the edge of the stream and took out his last sandwich. Just then he saw a fish swimming by.

'P'raps you're the one who is going to help me,' he said, and threw the last sandwich into the water. But the fish dodged under a stone and the sandwich floated away down the stream.

George jumped up and followed the bobbing sandwich to see where it would go. Soon the stream widened and ran into a pool, and there on the bank stood a big boy watching a fishing-line.

'Don't make so much noise!' said the big boy. 'You'll frighten the fish away!'

'Sorry!' said George. 'Would you like some milk?' he asked.

'Milk? Are you off your head? How d'you expect me to drink milk while I'm fishing? You scram out of here and be quick about it!'

Well, there was nothing for it; George had to make himself scarce, but he was beginning to feel a little sad. His adventure wasn't turning out quite as he had planned. He sat down in a patch of bilberries and drank up his bottle of milk himself. Then he lay down and took a little nap.

When he woke up there was a little girl standing there, watching him.

'Hullo!' said George.

'Hullo!' said the little girl. 'You looked so nice, lying there asleep; just like my cousin! What a smart sandwich tin you've got; I haven't got one like that with Donald Duck on it.'

'Got it for my birthday,' said George. He was suddenly feeling very hungry, but there was nothing left to eat.

'Are you hungry?' asked the little girl. 'I can give you some food, if you like. I'm bilberrying, you see, so I've brought a picnic lunch—look! Sausages and strawberry jelly; it's jolly good!'

'Thank you very much,' said George, and he ate up two sausages and all the jelly that was left.

The little girl stood watching him, and when he had finished she said, 'Now you will have to save me from the dragon.'

'Dragon?' George gulped and the last bit of jelly went down the wrong way.

'Of course,' she said. 'When you've eaten the princess's food you must kill the dragon. It is lying just down there in the bushes.'

'All right, I'm ready!' said George in his most manly

voice. He was a *little* afraid when he started walking over to the bushes. But he picked up a good stout stick—sorry, I mean sword—and smacked the dragon right on the nose. Wham! Afterwards he hacked it into several pieces and then he jumped on them to make quite sure it was dead.

'It's quite safe now, Princess!' he said to the little girl. 'You can come out now!'

'Oh, thank you, St George!' she said. 'Now you can

marry me if you like—unless I marry my cousin, of course.'

'You marry your cousin,' said George. 'I don't mind.'

'All right. But you can come home with me if you like, and have some more jelly.'

'No thanks, Princess,' said George. 'You see, I have to look for the gold now that I've killed the dragon.'

And do you know? Under the tree-stump—sorry, I mean the dragon—George found a heap of beautiful pebbles that shone in the sun like silver when he ran them through his hands. George put them all in his knapsack and was very pleased with his treasure even though it wasn't gold.

After all, you can't expect to find gold under the first dragon that you kill.

The Ski-Race

MRS PEPPERPOT has done a lot of things in her life, and most of them I've told you about already. But now I must tell you how she went ski-racing one day last winter.

*   *   *   *   *

Mr Pepperpot had decided to go in for the annual local ski-race. He had been a pretty good skier when he was young, so he said to Mrs Pepperpot:

'I don't see why I shouldn't have a go this year; I feel more fit than I have for many years.'

'That's right, husband, you do that,' said Mrs Pepperpot, 'and if you win the cup you'll get your favourite ginger cake when you come home.'

So Mr Pepperpot put his name down, and when the day came he put on his white anorak and blue cap with a bobble on the top and strings under his chin. He slung his skis over his shoulders and said he would wax them when he got to the starting point.

'Righto! Best of luck!' said Mrs Pepperpot. She was already greasing the cake-tin and stoking the stove for her baking.

'Thanks, wife,' said Mr Pepperpot and went off. It was not before he had turned the corner by the main road that Mrs Pepperpot caught sight of his tin of wax which he had left on the sideboard.

'What a dunderhead that man is!' exclaimed Mrs Pepperpot. 'Now I shall have to go after him, I suppose; otherwise his precious skis are more likely to go backwards than forwards and there'll be no cup in this house today.'

So Mrs Pepperpot flung her shawl round her shoulders and trotted up the road as fast as she could with the tin of wax. When she got near the starting point there was a great crowd gathered. She dodged in and out to try and find her husband, but everyone seemed to be wearing white anoraks and blue caps. At last she saw a pair of sticks stuck in the snow with a blue cap hanging from the top. She could see the initials P.P. sewn in red thread inside.

'That must be his cap,' thought Mrs Pepperpot. 'Those are his initials, Peter Pepperpot. I sewed them on myself in red thread like that. I'll just drop the wax in the cap; then he'll find it when he comes to pick up his sticks.'

As she bent forward to put the wax in the cap she accidentally knocked it off the stick and at that moment

46

she shrank so quickly that it was she who fell into the cap, while the tin of wax rolled out into the snow!

'No harm done,' thought Mrs Pepperpot; 'when he comes along he'll see me in his cap. Then he can put me down somewhere out of the way of the race. And as soon as I grow large again I can go home.'

But a moment later a big hand reached down, snatched up the cap and crammed it over a mop of thick hair. The strings were firmly tied and Mrs Pepperpot was trapped!

'Oh well!' she thought. 'I'd better not say anything before the race starts.' For she knew Mr Pepperpot hated to think anybody might get to know about her shrinking.

'Number 46!' she heard the starter shout, 'on your mark, get set, go!' And Number 46, with Mrs Pepperpot in his cap, glided off to a smooth start.

'Somebody must have lent him some wax,' she thought; 'there's nothing wrong with his skis, anyway.' Then from under the cap she shouted, 'Don't overdo it, now, or you'll have no breath left for the spurt at the end!'

She could feel the skier slow up a little. 'I suppose you know who's under your cap?' she added. 'You had forgotten the wax, so I brought it along. Only I fell into your cap instead of the wax.'

Mrs Pepperpot now felt the skier's head turn round to see if anyone was talking to him from behind.

'It's me, you fool!' said Mrs Pepperpot. 'I've shrunk again. You'll have to put me off by the lane to our house—you pass right by, remember?'

But the skier had stopped completely now.

'Come on, man, get a move on!' shouted Mrs Pepperpot. 'They'll all be passing you!'

'Is it . . . is it true that you're the little old woman who shrinks to the size of a pepperpot?'

'Of course—you know that!' laughed Mrs Pepperpot.

'Am *I* married to *you*? Is it *my* wife who shrinks?'

'Yes, yes, but hurry now!'

'No,' said the skier, 'if that's how it is I'm not going on with the race at all.'

'Rubbish!' shouted Mrs Pepperpot. 'You *must* go on! I put a cake in the oven before I went out and if it's scorched it'll be all your fault!'

But the skier didn't budge.

'Maybe you'd like me to pop out of your cap and show myself to everybody? Any minute now I might go back to my full size and then the cap will burst and the whole crowd will see who is married to the shrinking woman. Come on, now! With any luck you may just do it, but there's no time to lose; HURRY!'

This worked; the skier shot off at full speed, helping himself to huge strides with his sticks. 'Fore!' he shouted as he sped past the other skiers. But when they came to the refreshment stall Mrs Pepperpot could smell the lovely hot soup, and she thought her husband deserved a break. 'We're well up now,' she called. 'You could take a rest.'

The skier slowed down to a stop and Mrs Pepperpot could hear there were many people standing round him. 'Well done!' they said. 'You're very well placed. But what are you looking so worried about? Surely you're not frightened of the last lap, are you?'

'No, no, nothing like that!' said the skier. 'It's this cap of mine—I'm dead scared of my cap!'

But the people patted him on the back and told him not to worry, he had a good chance of winning.

Under the cap Mrs Pepperpot was getting restless again. 'That's enough of that!' she called. 'We'll have to get on now!'

The people who stood nearest heard the voice and wondered who spoke. The woman who ladled out the soup said, 'Probably some loud-speaker.'

And Mrs Pepperpot couldn't help laughing. 'Nearer the truth than you think!' she thought. Then she called out again, 'Come on, husband, put that spurt on, and let's see if we can make it!'

And the skis shot away again, leaping many yards each time the sticks struck into the snow. Very soon Mrs Pepperpot could hear the sound of clapping and cheering.

'What do we do now?' whispered the skier in a miserable voice. 'Can you last another minute? Then I can throw the cap off under the fir trees just before we reach the finishing line.'

'Yes, that will be all right,' said Mrs Pepperpot. And, as the skis sped down the last slope, the strings were untied and the cap flew through the air, landing safely under the fir trees.

When Mrs Pepperpot had rolled over and over many times she found herself growing big once more. So she got up, shook the snow off her skirt and walked quietly home to her house. From the cheering in the distance she was sure her husband had won the cup.

The cake was only a little bit burnt on the top when she took it out of the oven, so she cut off the black part and gave it to the cat. Then she whipped some cream to put on top and made a steaming pot of coffee to have ready for her champion husband.

Sure enough, Mr Pepperpot soon came home—

without the cup. 'I forgot to take the wax,' he said, 'so I didn't think it was worth going in for the race. But I watched it, and you should have seen Paul Petersen today; I've never seen him run like that in all my born days. All the same, he looked very queer, as if he'd seen a ghost or something. When it was over he kept talking about his wife and his cap, and he wasn't satisfied till he'd telephoned his house and made sure his wife had been there all the time, watching the race on television.'

Then Mrs Pepperpot began to laugh. And ever since, when she's feeling sad or things are not going just right, all she has to do is to remember the day she went ski-racing in the wrong cap, and then she laughs and laughs and laughs.